The Indian Imagination of Girish Karnad

Essays on *Hayavadana*

The Indian Imagination of Girish Karnad

Essays on *Hayavadana*

P. DHANAVEL

PRESTIGE

Published by

PRESTIGE BOOKS

3/28, East Patel Nagar

New Delhi 110 008

2009

Rs. 400
Prestige Books
International

ISBN: 81-7551-077-3

Composed by Vivek Mathur, Delhi 110 006 Ph. 3981867

Printed by Dhawan Industries Offset, New Delhi 110 028

CONTENTS

Foreword

The book entitled *The Indian Imagination of Girish Karnad* is a critical study of the pre-eminent contemporary play-wright Girish Karnad with special reference to *Hayavadana.* The first chapter brings out the dramatist's humanistic vision and provides the background for the whole study. Then, the following five chapters analyze the various complex facets of *Hayavadana,* namely identity crises, anxiety of influence, the transformation of Shakuntala into Padmini and Hayavadana, condensation, and desire for recognition. Ex-amining the distinguishing characteristics of Karnad's Indian imagination, the last chapter projects *Hayavadana* as Kar-nad's most representative play.

A serious assessment of Karnad's dramatic output in his own English translation upto now, this book will be a mile-stone in Karnad scholarship and criticism. I hope that it will be useful to the teachers, research scholars and students of literature who are interested in understanding and appreciating Indian society and culture, as it highlights the perennial psy-cho-socio-political problems embedded in Karnad's plays.

Dr. P. Dhanavel, Department of English, Tripura Uni-versity, is a well-known scholar, teacher and critic. I have every hope that *The Indian Imagination of Girish Karnad* written by him will be received well by its readers.

PROFESSOR A.K. CHAKRABORTY
Vice-Chancellor
Tripura University

For my grandmother

Preface

Over ten years ago I had a vague impression that Girish Karnad's *Hayavadana* was a play of some great magnitude. Then I could only feel it but now I have given a critical account of my impression. The subsequent plays *Naga-Mandala, Tale-Danda* and *The Fire and the Rain* have rather strengthened my initial assumption.

Especially, *Hayavadana* gives expression to the Indian imagination in its richest colours and profound meanings. Hence, this volume progresses from humanism through identity crisis, anxiety of influence, literary genetics, condensation, and desire for recognition to the Indian imagination. The students and teachers of literature, sociology, psychology and cultural anthropology will find these explorations useful in enhancing their understanding and appreciation of Indian literature and society.

A great deal of debt I owe to many friends and well-wishers all over the country for their kind help at various stages. Dr. Noel Irudayaraj, Dr. A. Joseph and Dr. Premakumari Marshall of Bharathidasan University initiated me into the mysteries of *Hayavadana*. Dr Sukhbir Singh and Dr. Tutun Mukherjee of Osmania University accepted my paper on "The Romance of Influence" for their seminar on Critical, Literary and Social Theory at ASRC, Hyderabad, and later published it in the special issue of *Indian Journal of Ameri-*

can Studies (1993). Dr. Ravi Nandan Sinha included the essay on "A Study in Condensation" in *The Quest* (1997). Dr. M.K. Pandey of Purvanchal University published the paper on "The Humanistic Vision" in his collection of essays *Contemporary Indian Literature in English.* Professor C.D. Narasimhaiah encouraged me to write the essay on "The Indian Imagination" for his seminar on the Makers of Indian English at Dhvanyaloka, though I could not present it in person. The rest I have written for this volume.

It is my privilege to acknowledge the assistance I have received from the libraries and the staff of various institutions across the country: National College, Holy Cross College, Bharathidasan University, Tiruchirappalli; Study Centre for Indian Literature in English and Translation, American College, Madurai, University of Madras, Chennai; Jawaharlal Nehru University, New Delhi; American Studies Research Centre, Hyderabad; Tripura University, Maharaja Bir Bikram College, Bir Chandra State Central Library, Agartala. The number of individuals who helped me in one way or another is too large to be mentioned here, though I remember them all with gratitude on this occasion. I record my gratitude to Professor A.K. Chakraborty for his kind foreword.

Finally, I wish to thank Dr. R.K. Dhawan who kindly sent me a copy of *The Plays of Girish Karnad* and enabled me to prepare the final manuscript. Prestige Books deserves a special word of thanks for bringing out this book to the benefit of a wide audience.

P. DHANAVEL

The Humanistic Vision of Girish Karnad

By dint of his own outstanding dramatic genius Girish Karnad has emerged as the most significant playwright of the post-Independence Indian literature. His plays, first written in Kannada and then translated into other languages, including English, have brought him national and international recognition in several ways. Both theatre and drama critics have heaped praises on Karnad while appreciating many aspects of his plays: plot construction, characterization, song, spectacle, symbolism, use of myths and folktales, reinterpretation of history, highlight on contemporary, social, and psychological problems, especially those of women and children, sources and influences, technical innovations and so forth.

In the past four decades since *Yayati* (1961), however, the humanistic vision of Karnad, though it is central to his plays as it is in other Indian writers, seems to have received little critical notice, not because it did not warrant special attention but because of the initial problems of the emerging post-Independence Indian literature like the medium and the stage. An attempt is made here to bring out the humanistic vision of Girish Karnad with reference to the plays that he himself has translated into English: *Tughlaq*, *Hayavadana*, *Naga-Mandala*, *Tale-Danda*, and *The Fire and the Rain*.

Humanism is an umbrella term covering a wide range of connotations. To begin with, it refers to the philosophical outlook fathered by Protagoras, a fifth century B.C. Greek sophist, who is credited with the central tenet, "Man is the measure of all things." However, this point of view gathered momentum only when Petrarch, a fourteenth century Italian poet and scholar initiated the process of Renaissance to break away from the medieval clutches. Gradually, Renaissance humanism, which was compatible with the contemporary religious beliefs and practices, became very popular throughout Europe. Shakespeare, for instance, was as great a humanist as Erasmus, More and Montaigne were.

Second, humanism denotes classicism because the original humanists invariably returned to the ancient Greek and Roman thinkers for inspiration and revitalization of intellectual pursuit. Third, it signifies the humanities, including language, literature, rhetoric, philosophy, and art history. In this sense, it is opposed to the sciences as they are taught and studied in the universities and colleges, Fourth, it suggests anthropocentrism, that is, human-centredness. Protagoras's pithy saying is usually considered to indicate man's supremacy over nature. Nevertheless, human-centredness is only "axiological" and not "factual," as pointed out by D.D. Bandiste (15).

Fifth, any return to the past in general is deemed to be humanistic. A notable instance is the New Humanism of Irving Babbitt and Paul Elmer More of the United States, who, in the early twentieth century, emphasized a universal scale of ethical values transcending specific societies. According to M.H. Abrams (84), the New Humanism marked a decisive return to the Greek reason, the Christian restraint and the Oriental compassion. Sixth, a variety of pragmatism practised by the English pragmatist Ferdinand Schiller is called humanism, for he believed that man was the creator of truth.

Seventh, the humanistic ethical, political and social ideals were incorporated with Christianity, giving rise to a brand of religious humanism known as Christian humanism. The French theologian Jacques Maritain is a famous Christian humanist of this century. Eighth, antithetical to religious humanism is positioned secular humanism which is adhered to by most of the materialists, scientists, agnostics and others. In its radical forms, secular humanism aims at eradicating all kinds of superstitious and supernatural beliefs as well as practices which obstruct rather than facilitate the progress of general human welfare. Among a host of other connotations, the most significant variety of humanism points to certain cherished human ideals and values such as understanding, benevolence, compassion, mercy, fortitude, judgment, eloquence, love of honour, liberty, equality, fraternity, democracy and social justice.

The late twentieth century is, however, characterized by an interrogation of all human ideas and ideals from the structuralists, poststructuralists, and postmodernists who are perceived as anti-humanists, though the thoroughgoing interrogative spirit is an essential aspect of all humanistic thought. Thus, the course of humanism displays often conflicting and contradictory views, but all of them are equally concerned with the question of man and his place in the universe.

In view of the differing meanings of humanism, some important critical questions issue forth at this juncture. In what sense is Girish Karnad a humanist? What does he seek to project for humanity through his plays? To answer these questions satisfactorily, it is worthwhile to see beforehand the playwright's personal, familial, educational, social, political and historical background.

It is widely known that Karnad is a multifariously talented personality. First and foremost, he is a playwright. As Geetha Sharma (1998:5) reports: "it is playwriting that he has really enjoyed all along, and will undoubtedly be remembered by posterity for." So far he has written only nine plays and most of them are highly successful both on stage and among literary critics: *Yayati* (1961), *Tughlaq* (1964), *Hayavadana* (1971), *Anjumallige* (1977), *Hittina Hunja* (1980), *Naga-Mandala* (1988), *Tale-Danda* (1990), *Agni Mattu Malle* (1995), and *Dreams of Tipu Sultan* (1998). Persuaded by somebody or the other, he has also translated many of his plays into English. Further, he has extended his translation activity to plays by his contemporaries, notably Badal Sircar and Vijay Tendulkar. Besides, he has written with great acumen on Indian theatre. His essay "Theatre in India," for example, will remain a landmark in Indian theatre and drama criticism for years to come.

Devoted to drama as Karnad was, he had to turn to other fields for earning a livelihood. As soon as he returned from England after the period of his Rhodes Scholarship at Oxford, he joined Oxford University Press, Madras, as an assistant manager. His stay there proved to be fruitful for him in more than one way. He could actively participate in the Madras Players group as an actor, a playwright and a director. He could also publish his plays in English from Oxford India. After he rose to the position of Manager, Oxford University Press, he went to Pune as the Director of Film and Television Institute of India. From there, it was easy for him to get into the popular Hindi films. Action, Direction, Script Writing all came as grist to his mill. He did not leave the small screen either. He appeared in several T.V. serials, including R.K. Narayan's *Malgudi Days*. He continues to turn up on the T.V. for the weekly "Turning Point" programme among others. He has held important administrative posts like the chairmanship of Sangeet Natak Akademi and Children's Film Society. The awards and fellowships that he has received over the years are too numerous to be recorded here. Mention, however, may be made of the Fulbright Fellowship, and the Sahitya Akademi Award and the Jnanpeeth Award. A succinct account of the man and the writer Karnad is provided by R.K. Dhawan (11-20). Such a versatile personality like the ideal Renaissance man cannot but be a humanist.

Born at Matheran near Bombay in 1938, Karnad hails from the semi-Marathi and semi-Kannada Saraswat community (Murthy 1995: 137). While growing up in Sirsi, he had ample opportunity for watching plays in Kannada, the language that he later chose to write his plays in. He used to go to Company Natak performances with his father, who, being a doctor, had a free pass. As his parents considered *Yakshagana* performances inferior to their taste, the young Karnad went to such plays with the servants (Karnad 1989a: 85-87). The technical aspects of these two varieties of drama have, obviously, gone into the making of Karnad's plays, though he has imbibed the best from the Western theatre too. Since his father was an Arya Samajist (Raykar 339), Karnad did not have the orthodox way of life. For this precise reason, he is often drawn to the orthodox forms of life, especially those of the high caste, in his plays and films. In his early life, however, he had a serious ambition to become a famous poet in English but to his dismay he turned out to be a dramatist, but not in his mother tongue which is Konkani.

Just as the personal and family background of Karnad is essential for understanding his humanistic vision, it is necessary to have a picture of the socio-politico-historical context in which he began to write his plays. In the "Author's Introduction" to *Three Plays*, Karnad (1995:1) observes:

> My generation was the first to come of age after India became Independent of British rule. It therefore had to face a situation in which tensions implicit until then had come out in the open and demanded to be resolved without apologia or self-justification: tensions between the cultural past of the country and its colonial past, between the attractions of Western modes of thought and our own traditions, and finally between the various visions of the future that opened up once the common cause of political freedom was achieved.

With political freedom did not come the personal and human freedom to all citizens. While the people were yet to feel themselves independent, the Indian leaders went ahead with their grandiose plans of national development and reconstruction, but their unscrupulous followers went along with their counter-plans of selfish development. The net result was complete disenchantment with the independent India, which has taken alarming proportions today. The noble ideals of patriotism, liberty, equality, justice, and so on were thrown to the winds. Consequently, every sensitive artist reacted to the depressive and oppressive environment in his own way. Karnad's deeply humanistic responses are reflected in all his plays. His latest play *Dreams of Tipu Sultan*, in fact, commemorates the Golden Jubilee of Indian Independence.

The salient features of Karnad's humanism as derived from a bio-critical study are: (a) a profound concern for man, especially the oppressed and the downtrodden, (b) a compulsive return to and reinterpretation of the past mythical, historical, and oral stories, (c) a determined demystification of the dominant beliefs and practices, both secular and spiritual, (d) a sympathetic understanding and affirmation of this physical and earthly life, and (e) an incisively insightful contemporary social relevance. These humanistic characteristics are unfolded in all his plays. Nevertheless, the plays in his own English translation, *Tughlaq*, *Hayavadana*, *Naga-Mandala*, *Tale-Danda*, and *The Fire and the Rain* are discussed here with a special emphasis on *Hayavadana*.

There is a pervasive and profound concern for man in Karnad's plays. It is not, however, a reduplication of Protagoras's theory, nor of Francis Bacon's praxis. Hence, Karnad's humanism is not strictly anthropocentric. He does not believe that the world has been created for man to conquer and abuse it. To be precise, what Karnad aims at is an ecological vision in which man and all creatures as well as inanimate objects would live in coexistence. He has projected such a view in his telefilm *Cheluvi*. Clearly, the message is that no one can live by destruction, enmity, hatred, ill-will, and so on. With this deep understanding, Karnad has directed his attention to the helpless, the trapped, the inarticulate, the handicapped, the oppressed, the downtrodden, the neglected, the exploited, and the abused in the ladder of existence, and argued dramatically for a better world, though he is aware of the perenniality of human problems.

In the maniacal pursuit of his utopia, Tughlaq clears the ground ruthlessly until he is shamed on his face by the poor dhobi Aziz. *Tughlaq* is a tragedy, a satirical tragedy at that, but the existential humanistic outlook of Karnad is etched on every page from the beginning to the end through several characters: the old man, the Hindu, Aziz, Aazam, the Stepmother, Najib, Barani, Sheikh Imam-ud-din, the starved crowd, the young soldier, and so forth. The scholarly historian Barani's perspective on Aziz is proved wrong when Aziz is pardoned by the Sultan. Even Tughlaq, who is madly merciless, receives the most sympathetic treatment from Karnad. Similarly, the sad plights of the Man, the Flame, the Story, Rani, Kurudavva, and Kappanna in *Naga-Mandala* are brought on to the stage vividly, emphasizing Karnad's genuine feeling for the ignorant men and women and their place in the universe. The second ending of *Naga-Mandala* has an empathetic concern for the Cobra, which is then revived and recoiled in the tresses of Rani as a burden worth carrying for life. Who else other than Karnad will have such extraordinary love for the usually contemptible and frightful creatures?

As Tughlaq strikes the chord of sympathy for the whole country, *Tale-Danda* rings the bell of awareness for the whole society, which is ever torn by caste conflicts. Surely, Basavanna's revolutionary movement for the casteless society of *sharanas* is almost as utopian as Tughlaq's for a liberal, fraternal, and egalitarian country. Even though Basavanna is tactful enough, he could not prevent the tragedy ensuing the intercaste marriage. Worse, the whole fabric of Basavanna's movement is destroyed when his extremist follower Jagadeva kills Bijjala wantonly. Oppression and suppression continue more vehemently as soon as Sovideva ascends the throne. Likewise, *The Fire and the Rain* takes up complex issues and situations for revealing how the high caste feeds upon itself. The outcaste Arvasu is prevented from marrying the hunter girl Nittilai by Yavakri who spends ten years for achieving universal knowledge from Lord Indra only to seduce Vishakha, the wife of Paravasu, who is the Chief Priest at the Fire Sacrifice. Paravasu's father Raibhya too joins Yavakri in disturbing his son's ritualistic process by killing Yavakri with the Brahma Rakshasa. Consequently, Paravasu is forced to return home during the night and kill his own father. The action does not stop there. Paravasu throws the blame of patricide on his brother Arvasu and finally enters the fire when he has no use for life. In all these cases, Karnad has done his best to give each his or her voice for revealing their humanity. The ultimate villain, Indra, the god of rains, too is dealt not with a thunderbolt but with the cordial feathers of Karnad's humaneness.

Of all the plays of Karnad, however, it is *Hayavadana* that represents and symbolizes the playwright's discerning analysis of human problems, encompassing both the pre- and post-marital stages, from choosing a husband or a wife, through giving birth to children, and giving up one's ghost. The portrayal of Padmini is astoundingly humanistic in itself, though the hybrid 'child' Hayavadana carries the weightage. His pathetic story is no doubt enchanting but his questions are more enlightening. His end is ridiculous enough but he leaves the stage with rich thoughts for a more enduring positive attitude to life. It is he who asks more questions and represents everyman's predicament of the search for unattainable perfection more dramatically and authentically. The fact that his is a story invented by Karnad himself for the purpose of double perspective is indicative of the playwright's profound concern for the imperfect mortal called man.

Unlike the leading contemporary playwrights Badal Sircar and Vijay Tendulkar, Karnad has compulsively returned to the past mythical, historical and oral tales for his themes as well as characters and situations. The *Mahabharata* alone is a source for two of his complex plays. While his first play *Yayati* is from the *Adiparva*, the first book of the epic, his latest play *The Fire and the Rain* is from the *Vanaparva*, the third book of the same epic. *Hayavadana* is also indirectly indebted to the *Mahabharata* for the episode of the abandoned child, that is, Shakuntala. The myth of king Yayati appealed to the young Karnad because it gave expression to his own feeling of being deprived by the paternal authority. When Yayati was cursed with old age, he transferred it to his son Puru, who was born of Sharmishtha. Consequently, Puru fails as a husband for Chitralekha who commits suicide owing to her husband's irresponsible and callous behaviour. Thus, the episode of Yayati is useful in bringing out the theme of responsibility in the modern context. Paternal loyalty is a fine gesture but it can be ruinous in the nuclear family today, when it is misappropriated.

According to Karnad, *The Fire and the Rain* is the "most complex" (Sharma 1998: 6) play up to now. The play is based on the myth of Yavakrita but the psychological motives of Paravasu, Arvasu, and Raibhya are explored logically to the limitations of all forms of approaches to god. Interestingly, Karnad adds the beautiful creature Nittilai as well as the play-within-the-play. It has the Shakespearean echoes of Hamlet and his play. Paravasu reacts to Arvasu's play as Gertrude does to Hamlet's. While Hamlet dies tragically, Arvasu is honoured by the sudden appearance of Lord Indra to grant him any boon which he uses for releasing the tormented soul of the Brahma Rakshasa, a strange but invisible demon. Unlike Ophelia who drowns herself, Nittilai is killed by her own husband. All along Karnad has seriously attempted to overcome his anxiety of influence. *The Fire and the Rain* is certainly Karnad's challenge to Shakespeare's *Hamlet* as *Hayavadana* is to Kalidasa's *Shakuntala*.

If *Yayati* and *The Fire and the Rain* are mythical plays, *Tughlaq, Tale-Danda,* and *Dreams of Tipu Sultan* are historical plays which are derived from Indian history. Significantly, both *Tughlaq* and *Dreams of Tipu Sultan* are concerned with the Mughal kings. While the former deals with the panoramic fourteenth century Indian history, the latter focusses on the oppressive eighteenth century Mysore history. Both plays attempt to highlight the gap between the dreams and deeds of the two greatest kings who began with the noble aim of building a glorious kingdom but ended up in gory violence. If Tughlaq had to contend with his Muslim enemies, Tipu had to fight with the British forces. The Muslims gave way to the British imperial raj. Strikingly, *Tale-Danda* presents a more gruesome aspect of Indian history and society. The twelfth century saint Basavanna from the city of Kalyan in Karnataka was no less a dreamer. He imagined a casteless society and succeeded in creating such a society, though it failed. These three historical figures have interested Karnad for the complexity of the problems that they faced. As Karnad tries to understand why they did not succeed, he is able to bring to the audience the relevance of the problems which made their heroic tragedies.

Hayavadana and *Naga-Mandala* are tales drawn from the written and oral traditions, respectively. These folk tales offer adequate scope for Karnad's dramatic imagination to weave his humanistic vision about the down-to-earth aspect of human life. *Naga-Mandala* is shaped from two Kannada stories that Karnad had heard from A.K. Ramanujan in Chicago. The preliminary story of the Man and the Flames is the outer frame for the main story of Rani. In a sense, this play is a direct offshoot of *Hayavadana*. Devadatta and Kapila kill each other for the sake of Padmini whereas Naga saves Rani from the trial and sacrifices himself for the happiness of Rani and Appanna. Besides, like Hayavadana, Naga stands for a more genuine humanism than the human beings themselves. If the Story of the Flames emphasizes the values of stories in their telling and listening, the Story of Rani suggests that these stories of values are fictional but foundational for human life. What is exceptional about *Hayavadana* is that Karnad makes a transnational use of the mythical story of *Vetalapanchavimsati* via Thomas Mann's long story "The Transposed Heads." Additionally, he has invented the whole sub-plot of Hayavadana and entitled the play after this mixed creature. While the main story of Devadatta, Kapila and Padmini has a social dimension of one woman and two men with whom Karnad has had personal acquaintance, the secondary story of Hayavadana fulfils the playwright's ambition to write a play with sub-plot like Shakespeare's *King Lear*. The latter story is also a symptom of the fact that Karnad was "unconsciously overcoming my own resistance to the use of masks." (Paul 4) The deep roots for both plots, however, lie in Kalidasa's *Shakuntala* as well as the episode of Shakuntala in the *Mahabharata*, for these sources illuminate the status of abandoned children and their callous parents.

The thoroughgoing interrogative spirit of the humanist does not leave any belief or practice unchallenged. In his plays, Karnad questions all kinds of superstitious and supernatural beliefs and practices, both secular and spiritual, directly as well as indirectly. A certain amount of skepticism, even bordering on cynicism runs through the tragic, pathetic, comic, and ludicrous characters and situations. Consequently, Karnad has come to depend heavily on irony at the conceptual and technical level, achieving incredible dramatic scores. A truthfully Indian dramatist, Karnad engages, in the existential sense of the term, the dominant and destructive notions of caste and religion in all his plays. For, a Hindu is born in a caste, in a language, in a thinking pattern, and in an occupation. Karnad, then, re-creates the Indian society in his plays to uncover the layers of false beliefs and practices one after another rigorously and relentlessly. Some critics like A.R. Shukla (289-94) use the term deconstruction to describe Karnad's dramatic enterprise. However, demystification seems to be a much better alternative, as it does not imply the abyss of endless signification that Derrida has attributed to deconstruction.

Plays like *Yayati, Tughlaq, Hittina Hunja*, and *Tale-Danda* that deal extensively with kings tear the idea of kingship to shreds. In the name of his kingdom, Yayati wants to hold on to the throne at the cost of his own son Puru's personal life. Likewise, Tughlaq brings about destruction in his kingdom through his imaginary and impracticable dreams of utopia. Behind each of his dreams lies a political and strategic motif. He depends on the Hindus and wants unity more for warding off the threats from the Muslims. Clever and cunning Muslims like Aziz fully exploit Tughlaq's plans for their own profit. The real sufferers are the common Muslims and the Hindus. Even the most sacred religious institution, prayer, is not left untouched by the power-mongers, including the king. Naturally, a number of critics (Bhatta 191, Gopalie 7, Gowda 6, Murthy 1983: ix, Nayak 1983: 2-4, Ramamurthi 20, Reddy 155, among others) have time and again pointed out how Karnad employs prayer ironically as a significant leitmotif in *Tughlaq*. Actually, this motif is found in one form or the other in all the plays of Karnad. As most profane activities are done during the prayer, it is made to lose its religious aura.

How a king is made and unmade by whom for whom and for what purpose is divulged in *Tale-Danda*, though the play's centre of focus is Basavanna and his *sharana* movement. Once the priestly class comes to know that Bijjala, the king, has extended support to the "unholy" marriage of Sheelavanta, a cobbler's son with Kalavati, a brahmin's daughter, Damodar Bhatta, the minister makes the weakling Sovideva the king and abdicates Bijjala cunningly. Though Bijjala realizes that god does not exist, he finds shelter in the god's room. Damodara Bhatta and his allies invoke the authority of god and scriptures to protect themselves. Basavanna admits that there was no miracle at the treasury, but the rumour becomes the truth. In *Hittina Hunja*, even a Jain king is motivated to misuse the sacred ritual to cover up his wife's adultery by committing cruelty in thought and in symbol. The sacrificial cock made of flour begins to crow just as it is going to be killed ritualistically.

The ritualistic processes meant for religious purposes are satirized in *Naga-Mandala* and *The Fire and the Rain* too. Rani becomes pregnant by Naga and proves her "innocence" by undertaking the Snake Ordeal which makes her a goddess instantly. Appanna, her husband, who ill-treated her until now, the elders of the village, and the others fall at Rani's feet and worship her. Though Appanna has his doubts, he can do nothing. In fact, he begins to suspect his own sanity, when the elders convince him that Rani is the Mother goddess. His own notions of the dominant male and the chaste wife are pulverized by the ironic situation. Thus, *Naga-Mandala* exposes the secular and spiritual maladies of the society.

The Fire and the Rain mocks at the chain of events leading to the arrival of Lord Indra and the rains. The King appoints Paravasu the chief priest of the yajna of seven years for bringing rains to his famine affected kingdom. But Paravasu's father Raibhya feels ignored and insulted. Similarly, Yavakri, Paravasu's cousin, also nurses feelings of frustration due to the neglect of his father. Hence, he does a rigorous tapasya for ten years to get Universal Knowledge from Lord Indra directly. He gets the knowledge but applies it for taking revenge on Paravasu. Therefore, he seduces Vishakha, Paravasu's wife, and throws the challenge which is answered immediately by Raibhya for disturbing his own son's fire sacrifice. Consequently, Paravasu comes home during the night against the established conventions and kills his father. The blame he throws upon his own brother Arvasu. Finally Lord Indra arrives on the scene pleased with

Arvasu's performance in the role of Vritya. As Arvasu releases the soul of the Brahma Rakshasa created by Raibhya to kill Yavakri, the rains start pouring down. The goodness in Arvasu is not nurtured by his family and tradition but by the hunter girl Nittilai who by her dedicated love saves the Actor-Manager, his family members, and also Arvasu, but dies in the process.

Demystification of religious beliefs and practices is at its height in *Hayavadana*. First, the incomplete and imperfect Lord Ganesha is ëxposed and then Hayavadana recounts his authentic experiences of wasteful pilgrimages that he had undertaken to all the holy places, holy people, gods and goddesses. Tirupati comes in for special criticism due to its celebrated hair offerings. His prayer to the Goddess at Mount Chitrakoot brings him more trouble than he has suffered so far. Finally, he is turned into a complete horse. His mother had also been changed into a mare by his celestial father. Clearly, then, the intervention of the supernatural beings in Hayavadana's life proves to be disastrous.

The ironic presentation of the most powerful Indian Goddess is the most deflating aspect of the play. Initially the Goddess is found sleeping, when both Devadatta and Kapila cut off their heads. She wakes up from her sleep when Padmini's turn for suicide comes. The Goddess puts all three unfortunate beings through a series of cruel difficulties and then finally drives them to their death. What is the nature of the Mother of all Nature then? This ironic presentation of the divine intervention negates the need for gods and goddesses. Thus, Karnad seems to suggest that it is better for human beings not to seek divine guidance because both the mediators and the divinities are sadistic and exploitative. Thus, *Tughlaq, Hayavadana, Naga-Mandala, Tale-Danda,* and *The Fire and the Rain* debunk the false structures of certain dominant beliefs and practices but affirm the reality of human life in its real motives.

Despite the serious doubts about the ends of human destiny, Karnad has accepted and affirmed the physical and earthly life. It has been possible for him mainly through his women characters in his plays. For, men in general tend to deny life in the interest of their dreams, visions and ideals. Therefore, women are usually considered as an enemy "out to spoil man" (Murthy 1995:135), though they are required for food and sex. As a result, women are not allowed to speak normally. They have relative freedom only when they fulfil these basic needs. According to Karnad, there are men who are willing to "abandon the food" also. He feels that these nuances of human relationships have to be brought into drama. Karnad's thoughts on these matters are close to the archetypal escape of the Americans to the wilderness, or the sea, or the river as shown by Leslie Fiedler in *Love and Death in the American Novel,* though without the male bondings that Fiedler identifies in the archetypal characters.

One of the earliest characters that Karnad invented is Chitralekha in *Yayati*. While Puru is great in sacrificing his youth for the sake of his father, he drives his wife Chitralekha to death. Both Puru and Yayati are mocked at for their ingenious notions by Chitralekha, when she commits suicide. She affirms life by her own death. For all its grand success, *Tughlaq* is lacklustre due to the absence of life-affirming women. Even Barani, the soft-hearted and sympathetic historian fails to evoke the desired response in Tughlaq and hence leaves him finally. Tughlaq's view of his mother and his stepmother clearly indicates the Fiedlerian character that he is. That is why he does not hesitate to stone his stepmother to death. Tughlaq is more or less manomaniacal like captain Ahab in the deadly pursuit of his dreams. He is wounded and so wounds unwaveringly all that come in his way.

Tale-Danda has nearly a dozen women characters and yet falls in the category of *Tughlaq* as it portrays Basavanna the saint. Though Gangambika, the saint's wife, is witty, lively and exuberant, she denies herself due to her husband. On the other hand, Savitri, Jagadeva's wife, is ill-treated cruelly. She is sent to her parents's home. When she comes back to help her mother-in-law, Jagadeva is angry with her. Amba, Bhagirathi, Kalyaṇi, Lalitha, Kalavati, and Rambhavati are too minor characters to make any impression at all. However, Lalitha dares defy the saint at one point and tells about the prophecy which comes true. She also reveals how her husband changed the religious wagons one after another. Interestingly, the courtesan Indrani is the audience for Damodara Bhatta to explain his theories of inequality. His king making process stands exposed by the presence of Indrani.

Unlike *Tughlaq* and *Tale-Danda, The Fire and the Rain, Naga-Mandala* and *Hayavadana* have strong women characters who also affirm life and give life to these plays. Both Vishakha and Nittilai in *The Fire and the Rain* exemplify the redeeming aspect of life. When Yavakri returns from his ten-year long tapasya, he is "hungry for words" (Karnad 1998:13) and finds his food in the loving and motherly woman Vishakha. She gives him herself but to her horror, he misuses her for his revenge on Paravasu. Nittilai is one of the most admirable characters of Karnad. She faces all sufferings for Arvasu and makes him a real human being with a better understanding of life. When Arvasu is obsessed with his revenge on Paravasu, she asks him, "Where will it end?" (43) and brings out the goodness in him. It is due to her influence that Arvasu releases the tormented soul of the Brahma Rakshasa, created by Raibhya to kill Yavakri. Nittilai's compassion is not confined to Arvasu alone. She is able to save the Actor-Manager and his family. She does not mind running around for food, medicine, and shelter, though she is aware that she is searched by her brother and husband. Finally, she is killed by her husband and even scolded by Arvasu for her goodness. Fortunately, she is followed by him to "where nothing matters, not your goodness, nor my stupidity, nor this world's evil." (58) But for Nittilai, Arväsu could have remained a Paravasu, a Raïbhya, or a Yavakri. It is for him and her, the rains come down at last.

Every hope of oppression has a ventilator of freedom. In *Naga-Mandala,* the woman who is locked up in the house all day and night finds fellowship and also freedom through Kurudavva, the blind woman, who gives some magic roots to Râni for winning her husband. It is with Kurudavva's intervention that Rani grows into a full woman by Naga. Rani does not understand what is happening until she feels her feet and that she is not dreaming any more. In fact, understanding is not a pre-requisite for affirming life. She is blessed enough to have a sympathetic Naga for loving and protecting her. Naga does not have to be seen as a man either. He is a symbol of fertility and Rani is the life principle. Both need to accept each other and procreate for the continuance of life. Not surprisingly, she emerges as the Mother goddess to bless her devotees, including her tyrannical husband and his concubine. The final note of forgiveness in Shakespeare's *The Tempest* is evident in *Naga-Mandala* as well as *The Fire and the Rain.*

Of all the women characters in Karnad, Padmini in *Hayavadana* is the most enchanting woman who wages a war against the patriarchal order of command and contentment. By her pungent honesty, she is able to achieve the impossible dream of a perfect man, though for a brief period. She walks out of her house with her son to the forest to seek Kapila, her dream rider. Though she falls a prey to the patriarchal society, she proves her worth and viewpoint before she enters the fire. She is as witty and vibrant as Gangambika, as courageous as Sharmishtha, as experimental as Rani, and as compassionate as Nittilai. She succumbs like Vishakha but does not allow herself to be abused and thrown away for the design of man. First, she is a challenge and then a dutiful wife to Devadatta. But her circumstance compels her to drift towards Kapila and then to mix up the heads of Devadatta and Kapila. She gets the fabulous brain and body but is soon disenchanted. Like Nittilai, she risks herself to make Kapila a complete man. What is noteworthy is that she does not deny the truth of her being, of her heart, and of her feeling. Whether or not Padmini continues to live happily ever after like Rani is immaterial for her purposes. She affirms her life in fire, when she cannot do it in rain. In this light, fire and rain attain the symbolic values of affirmation and negation. Surprisingly rain gives life but it corrupts the human heart. Therefore, fire is needed to burn up the corrupt heart for obtaining further life.

All the plays of Karnad have a remarkable contemporary social relevance, though he has invariably looked back to the distant past for themes. First, Karnad is attracted to the myths, histories, and folk stories for personal reasons. This autobiographical dimension is indubitably evident in *Yayati, Tughlaq* and *Hayavadana*. Next, he is excited by the universal characteristics of certain recurrent archetypes—problems, characters, situations, themes and so on. Hence, the personal and the social, the past and the present, commingle in Karnad's plays which will ever remain relevant to mankind.

In his "Author's Introduction" to *Three Plays*, Karnad states that he wrote *Yayati* "as an escape from my stressful situation" at the age of twenty, when he was going abroad for study. Similarly, *Tughlaq* too reflects a fear of failure that the playwright himself suffered from. In his interview with Rajinder Paul, he has confessed: "And I think basically as a person struggling against failure and failing more, somewhere must have found an immedidate echo in me." (3) Most importantly, the problems of faith in god that Tughlaq faced himself are reflected in all the plays of Karnad. *Hayavadana* too has a personal strain that he has related to Raykar (341). He has said that he was acquainted with the family of one woman and two men, one husband and another friend. The woman loved both of them and used to confuse their names, which is dramatized in the episode of the transposition of heads. Given the nature of Karnad's plays and his background, it is possible that the other plays too have such personal meaning for Karnad. However, the significant fact is that all his plays have a direct contemporary social relevance.

The contemporaneity of *Tughalq* was noticed by Karnad himself as he was choosing the subject for his play. Parallels between Tughlaq and Nehru were obvious, including the disenchantment that followed among the people. As U.R. Anantha Murthy remarks, *Tughlaq* is "more than a political allegory." (1983: viii) The murderous Najib has echoes of some of the later politicians. The numerous governmental schemes that are announced now and then and how they are implemented will always have memories of Tughlaq. Aziz's discovery of the political world in Delhi is currently relevant as the regional politicians have their field day in Delhi, threatening the government with withdrawal of support. The nexus between politicians and criminals as well as corrupt bureaucrats, and the unholy alliance between politicians and fake religious leaders are coming to the fore ever more. *Tughlaq*, then, is truly timeless.

Politics in India has always been caste politics. Unlike *Tughlaq*, *Tale-Danda* offers adequate scope for Karnad to explore the caste politics. In the Preface to the play, Karnad (1993) has said, "I wrote *Tale-Danda* in 1989 when the Mandir and Mandal movements were beginning to show again how relevant the questions posed by these thinkers were for our age." Basavanna, the twelfth century Kannada saint, believed that casteless society could be established and he did, but the caste system was too strong to be overthrown. This eternal problem distresses Karnad so much that he asks with anguish, "Why is that some of our problems seem perennial?" and further asks, "Why did Kabir not succeed?" (Chakravartee 49-50) The fact is that the kshatriyas need the brahmins for their support as the latter need the former. Monarchy has given way to democracy but it has proved a blessing for the high caste people to occupy positions of power for themselves. Though the system of government has changed, the caste system has not been removed from its hold. The recent developments in politics, especially after the Narasimha Rao government, speaks volumes for the deep concerns that Karnad has articulated in *Tale-Danda*.

Strangely, the power struggle within the brahminical circle is far worse than that between the various castes. *The Fire and the Rain* portrays how different brahmins, that too members of the same family, scheme against one another for the position of the chief priest at the fire sacrifice. The problem is that each one considers himself to be more knowledgeable than the other. Yavakri's father is supposed to be supreme but he has always been humiliated by Paravasu family. Raibhya is considered to be greater than his son Paravasu but the latter is chosen by the King as the Chief Priest. On the one hand, Yavakri takes revenge on Paravasu by seducing the latter's wife Vishakha. On the other, Raibhya wreaks vengeance on Paravasu by killing Yavakri. Worst of all, Paravasu kills his father and accuses Arvasu, his brother, of patricide, to continue as the Chief Priest. India is known for the learned rishis as well as the great power struggles among them. More than these, the intercaste marriage will ever remain a problem. Besides, the survival of playwrights, actors, and stage-managers has been a problem for centuries. As the Manager says, "a body needs to be fed before it can act" (Karnad 1998: 46). Karnad's own life is an example of this phenomenon. Through Arvasu, Karnad makes an important point that theatre has to be encouraged by the kings, that is, the state and central governments.

Naga-Mandala and *Hayavadana* fall under one group as they deal with the question of women's freedom. In *Naga-Mandala* Rani is married to Appanna but is deprived of her personal and familial needs. She is treated not even like a maid servant. She is locked in the house like a prisoner. She is, worse still, not allowed to speak with her husband by himself. When she attempts to communicate with Kurudavva, first a dog and then a mangoose guards her house. All this while, the husband lives with his concubine. By the strange magic of Kurudavva's roots, however, Rani gets the love and affection of Naga who also finally gives her freedom from oppression after the Snake Ordeal. Does the life of a woman have to be such an ordeal, Karnad seems to ask and to suggest that women's bodies cannot be kept in safety lockers, while the men can be thieves elsewhere. Perhaps, the matriarchal order may be conducive to both male and female.

The fullest expression to a woman's innermost feelings is given in *Hayavadana* through Padmini. A man can keep as many wives or mistresses as he likes but a woman is denied the same privilege. Does it mean that a woman does not have a desire for multiple husbands? The play answers the question affirmatively. Karnad aknowledges that a woman has her desire but cannot live like a Draupadi in the contemporary society. This problem is becoming more serious because women are more outgoing now. They tend to find their soul mates outside marriage and family. How are these women to live in the oppressive patriarchal society? When Padmini goes to the forest, Devadatta follows her with a sword in hand. Nittilai in *The Fire and the Rain* is also killed by her husband, when she walks out on him. Is the concept of *pativrata*, then, applicable to women like Padmini who die for two "husbands"? As a corollary, what will happen to the children born of such complicated relations?. Who will look after children like Hayavadana and Padmini's child? Do the parents have a right to leave their children to the vagaries of fate? Many such significant questions are raised in the play. Thus, each of Karnad's plays is relevant to the contemporary society.

Girish Karnad, then, is a humanist to the hilt. He is a humanist in the sense that he has a profound concern for both men and women, especially the oppressed and downtrodden. He is a humanist who believes in the past as a mirror for reflecting on the present and so has constantly turned to the past myths, histories, and oral tales for his themes. He is a humanist who is iconoclastic enough to demystify the dominant beliefs and practices, both secular and spiritual, that are more often put to evil use by the crooked and the biased. He is a humanist who affirms the physical and earthly life as it is, mainly through the indomitable women characters, as the men appear to negate life. No wonder, Karnad as a humanist has deep insight into the contemporary social and political problems, which are eternally relevant to mankind, though he does not openly suggest any pragmatic solutions for them. His humanistic solutions are implicitly embedded in the plays themselves. Karnad's humanism is tinged with a sense of loss, pain, suffering, incomprehension, and helplessness. The rebellious humanist however succeeds in making his voice heard. When the saint Basavanna and the saintly king Bijjala can be crucified, how can the society be redeemed? Questions like these are nailed fast to the readers and the audience of Karnad for ever.

The humanistic vision projected by Karnad is multidimensional and highly complex. There is something eccentric about the king in *Yayati* who does not like to shoulder his responsibility and shifts it to his son Puru. A megalomaniac halo surrounds the protagonist in *Tughlaq* as he keeps on employing various kinds of inhuman trickeries to keep himself in power. The sleepless playwright in *Naga-Mandala* and the starved Stage-Manager in *The Fire and the Rain* point to the society insensitive to the finer aspects of art, especially drama. Appanna remains a stranger to his wife Rani and almost turns a strangler whereas the husband of Nittilai ensures her death. A just attempt for a just and equal society is thwarted by the violent factions in *Tale-Danda*. The human reason seems to have no place in the human world, but then there is no other alternative for human problems.

Hayavadana occupies a unique status in the humanistic vision of Karnad. First, it encompasses three worlds of experience: the divine, the human and the animal. Within the human, the play includes the experiences of men, women, children as well as of the city and the wilderness. Second, the play presents the archetypal mother earth, teeming with desires for life and flowering the lotus of love for perfection and completeness. Third, Karnad's pro-vision of the child in the modern world is commendable. Despite his Brechtian alienation effects, sympathy is generated for Hayavadana who becomes a horse, and the child that learns to laugh. The tragedy of the adults is left behind and the comedy of the children is looked forward to. Though the irony is felt, the iron will of Karnad asserts itself giving the colour of hope to Karnad's humanistic vision.

What Karnad projects through his plays, especially *Tughlaq, Hayavadana, Naga-Mandala, Tale-Danda,* and *The Fire and the Rain,* is that human aspirations lead to inhuman desperations. Yayati, Tughlaq, Hayavadana, Padmini, Rani, Basavanna, Bijjala, Jagadeva, Arvasu, Nittilai, Yavakri and Vishakha are characters as well as situations depicting the road from beautiful imagination to harsh reality. Both the inner and outer world of man is ridden with psychological and social limitations. Being a thoroughgoing humanist, Karnad suggests that transcendence is possible only in immanence and believes that the generous acceptance of the tantalizing reality will be meaningful, even if the world remains terribly incomprehensible and inexplicable.

Identity Crisis in *Hayavadana*

In his "Introduction" to *Hayavadana*, Kirtinath Kurtkoti (1985: vi) has accurately remarked that the play deals with the problem of "human identity in a world of tangled relationships" causing "a confusion of identities which reveals the ambiguous nature of human personality" (Karnad 1995: 69-70). For, the play is chiefly concerned with the identity crises of Padmini in the main plot and of Hayavadana in the sub-plot. It is, then, worthwhile to explore the causes, complications, and climaxes of identity crisis in Girish Karnad's *Hayavadana* for a better understanding of the play as well as of the playwright.

The ancient Indian original of the main plot of *Hayavadana* is from *Vetalapanchavimsati*, a constituent of Somadeva's *Kathasaritsagara.* The Indian story is built upon the moral problem of deciding the identity of a woman's husband. A washerman marries a charming woman. They set out on a journey along with the woman's brother to participate in a festival in a nearby town. When they reach the Kali temple, the husband sacrifices his head to the Goddess. The woman's brother also offers his head to Kali. Left alone, the woman too prepares to kill herself but the Goddess prevents her from her suicidal attempt and helps her by reviving the dead. However, the anxious woman mixes up the heads. So, when the dead men wake up, the husband's head is on the brother's body and the brother's head on the husband's body. Now the difficult moral question is: Who is the woman's husband? The legendary wise king Vikram solves this problem by saying that the person who has the husband's head is the woman's husband because, according to him, a person's identity is determined by one's head. This is only one of the several versions of the story.

King Vikram's solution may be agreeable to the Indians. But a German like Thomas Mann, steeped in the Western view of the world, cannot accept it easily. Hence, he weaves a long short story called "The Transposed Heads" with a view to highlighting the philosophical problem of mind-body dualism. Being a materialist himself, Mann glorifies the body and suggests that it can be "a fit instrument for the fulfilment of human destiny" (69). Clearly, Mann uses the story as "a vehicle for the expression of his favourite idea, namely the ironic confrontation between opposites in human life" (Naik 1984:193).

While the Indian solution in *Vetalapanchavimsati* upholds idealism, the German solution in "The Transposed Heads" champions materialism. Aware of the extreme nature of these options, Karnad seems to hint at the middle course of humanism in *Hayavadana*. For, he dwells on the complex psycho-social dimensions of the problem of identity crisis. It is interesting to note, however, that he maintains the moral problem in the main plot and the philosophical problem in the sub-plot. He combines these two strands in the larger psycho-social plane of the concrete world for illuminating the essentially ambiguous nature of human personality. It is this intriguing and complex psycho-social dynamics of human identity crisis—a woman in love with two men (Raykar 342), the plight of abandoned children (Dhanavel 1997: 14-15) and the hierarchical social structure with all its repressive conventions (Murthy 1976: 42-43)—that lends charm to Karnad's play.

So long as Padmini remains "the daughter of the leading merchant in Dharmapura" (Karnad 1985:19), she has no problem whatsoever, not to speak of identity crisis. When she is passionately loved by Devadatta, the handsome and wise son of Vidyasagara of the same town, she gets into trouble with Kapila, the fast friend of Devadatta. It is not without significance, then, that her marriage with Devadatta is made possible by the active intervention of Kapila. The enviable friendship of Devadatta and Kapila flourishes as before and, in fact, leads to the acute crisis of identity in Padmini. For, there develops an undeclared and unconscious affinity between Padmini and Kapila. Consequently, Devadatta is mentally isolated from his wife and friend, though he loves both of them.

A day arrives when all the three go to the famous Ujjain fair. The beginning of the journey itself is complicated due to Devadatta's lack of serious interest in the fair. He likes to have the day for himself and his wife alone at home but Kapila is all set for the journey. The conflict in the mind of Padmini and her decisive attachment to Kapila are revealed at this stage. To please her husband, she at first says that the journey could be put off. On seeing the mental agony of Kapila, however, she changes her mind suddenly. Finally, they proceed on their disastrous journey.

On their way to Ujjain, they stop for a while in a forest to rest. Here again, Padmini's conflict is portrayed vividly. Now she no longer cares for her husband's hurt feelings and visits the Rudra temple along with Kapila. Of course, the social facade is maintained by Kapila who gets permission from Devadatta before departure. Sure of their mutual attraction, Devadatta remembers his vows to Lord Rudra and Goddess Kali, and goes to the deserted Kali temple to cut off his head. Disturbed by the absence of his friend, Kapila searches for him following the footprints. He too chops off his head for the sake of friendship. Padmini is disgusted with both of them. The inherent ambiguity in love, marriage, and friendship is brought out greatly in these circumstances. However, the identity crisis of Padmini is complicated further.

Conscious of the social stigma on her, Padmini too

reaches the Kali temple and gets ready to sever her head. At this juncture, Kali, who is sleeping, wakes up due to the noise made by Padmini. Initially, the Goddess is irritated but slowly comes forward to save Padmini from her critical situation. Granting Padmini's prayer for bringing back the dead men to life, the Goddess goes back to sleep. However, Padmini transposes the heads in her agitated state of mind. As a result, the identity of Devadatta and Kapilā becomes problematic. In fact, her own identity is at stake.

Two inter-related questions of identity crop up here: (a) Who is Padmini's husband? and (b) Whose wife is Padmini? The moral problem is solved by a learned rishi whose unequivocal verdict is reported by the Bhagavata: "As the heavenly Kalpa Vriksha is supreme among trees, so is the head among human limbs." Therefore, the man with Devadatta's head, is indeed, Devadatta and he is the rightful husband of Padmini (40). The verdict gives much happiness to both Padmini and Devadatta. She is overjoyed to have her "Fabulous body—fabulous brain—fabulous Devadatta" (43) and so is her revivified husband. Expectedly, Kapila is sad and parts company with them to live in the deep forest.

The moral problem of identity crisis is solved but not so is the psychological problem. Further biological transformations take place in both Devadatta and Kapila, as they reach their former self of distinct head and body. Gradually, Padmini is disenchanted with her transposed husband. In fact, she speaks to Devadatta about the increasing loss of Kapila's vitality in him. He brushes aside the question but she becomes obsessed with the memories of Kapila, which is dramaticaly well brought out through her song and the Dolls. She uses the Ujjain fair as an excuse to buy new dolls for their son and sends out the unwilling Devadatta. Then, she goes to the forest in search of Kapila and finds him at last. It is necessary to note that she also takes her son along with her. At first, Kapila is upset by Padmini's arrival but he accepts her to become a complete man himself, as suggested by Padmini. However, their happiness is short-lived, as Devadatta comes after them to put an end to their unsettled triangular life. Both Devadatta and Kapila realize that they love Padmini deeply but cannot live together "like the Pandavas and Draupadi" (60). Hence, they fight with each other and kill themselves. Padmini stands a mute spectator to this deadly fight because she also knows in her blood that they could not live together. Inevitably, she enters the funeral pyre as a sati. The identity crises of Padmini, of Devadatta as well as of Kapila lead all of them to find liberation in fire.

Karnad proleptically projects that Padmini needs "a man of steel." (19) Devadatta is not the man for her. Even the transposed Devadatta loses charm for her. The two men change to their "original self" but Padmini remains in her primordial procreative self. Karnad examines the psychological and sociological identity of these characters but has no method to cure them. Even as she enters the fire after the fashion of the typical Indian *pativrata*, Padmini is painfully aware of her identity crisis. She prays to her prototype: "Kali, Mother of all Nature, you must have your joke even now. Other women can die praying that they should get the same husband in all the lives to come. You haven't left me even that little consolation." (63) So dies Padmini as a discontented and deficient woman

If the tragic identity crisis of Padmini is presented in the main plot, the comic identity crisis of Hayavadana is unravelled in the sub-plot. Interestingly, Karnad invented the story of Hayavadana to solve his own identity crisis in his dramatic career. First, he wrote *Yayati* and then *Tughlaq*. Thereafter, he had hardly anything to do for playwriting. When he approached Mann's story, he had a plan to make a film. But his friend B.V. Karanth advised him to write a play. Then *Hayavadana* took shape in the form of a folk drama providing scope for Karnad to employ the double plot device successfully as Shakespeare had done in *Hamlet* and *King Lear* (Paul: 4). Karnad's creative identity crisis is explored elsewhere (Dhanavel 1993: 118-20). Suffice it to say that here Karnad has attempted to mollify his own dramatic identity crisis through Hayavadana, if not solve it completely. Karnad has not yet stopped his search for completeness (Ramnarayan 12-17).

The identity crisis of Hayavadana is physically manifest as an objective correlative for Padmini's; in a strange and distorted form, he has a horse's head on a human body. Quite strikingly, he is similar to Lord Ganesha "who has an elephant's head on a human body, a broken tusk and cracked belly" (1). If Hayavadana is seen as an unwelcome intruder into the main play, Lord Ganesha is brought to the stage as the supreme God. However, Hayavadana's interference is as meaningful as that of the presence of Ganesha, if not more. For instance, he is mistaken to have put on a mask by the Bhagavata who soon realizes that "this isn't a mask. It's his real head." (6) Then, mask is reality in the case of both Hayavadana and Ganesha. In contrast, the human beings exhibit no such correlation between appearance and reality.

Hayavadana's critical condition can be better understood in the light of his lineage. He is the offspring of a Celestial Being in the form of a horse and the Princess of Karnataka. Not surprisingly then, he is born with an equine head and a human body. Perhaps there is a biological association between male and head on the one hand, and female and body on the other. Such an association seems to be true in the case of Padmini's son who is as sulky and morose as his father but as lively and exuberant as his mother. Nevertheless, the sexual symbolism is obvious but it has a mythical base. After fifteen years of having the human love of the

Princess, the equine father becomes a celestial being who "had been cursed by the God Kubera to be born a horse for some act of misbehaviour." (8) He wants his wife to go with him to Heaven but she urges him to be the same horse. Exasperated, he curses her to be a horse and disappears. The cursed Princess joins the horse family. Only Hayavadana is left alone to search for his completeness. Not belonging to any group of his own is his problem of identity, but he is more than compensated with his intelligence.

Despite the physical identity crisis and the sense of alienation, Hayavadana seems to be superior to all the major and minor characters in the play. The horse head appears to symbolize plain common sense. He asks intelligent questions and points to several loopholes in the individual and social systems. His actual problem seems to be that he is not adequately aware of his superior intelligence. As a result, he is carried away by the deceptive figure of a complete man and is finally changed into a complete horse but with human voice by Goddess Kali's blessing of doubtful nature. Therefore, he has to worry his voice into singing the National Anthem. By a strange coincidence, he meets Padmini's son at the end of the play. It is during his amusing the little boy that Hayavadana loses his voice and starts neighing.

Could there be any suggestion that the common sense of Hayavadana is increased when he becomes a complete horse? Or could there be the opposite possibility that Hayavadana is deprived of his common sense after the change? If the latter is valid, the loss of Hayavadana's common sense is an irreparable loss for the country, for Indian drama, and for Karnad. Nothing like the extraordinary creature of Hayavadana has come out of Karnad either before or after *Hayavadana*. Of course, there is the Naga in *Naga-Mandala* but he is more a symbol of sexual energy than of common sense. As Karnad, and everybody, knows very well what is needed for a healthy society is pure horse sense and not the adulterated snake sense. Hayavadana's transformation, then, is sharply ironical.

Karnad has plainly suggested that reconciliation with one's self and one's environment is the best course of action for the incomplete and insatiable human beings. For the attempts of persons to achieve completeness and perfection usually end tragically and/or comically. However, the pathetic and ludicrous results are caused by certain external agents who may be described as supernatural beings, for they stand for superstitious beliefs, and not by the seekers themselves. An examination of the catalytic agents of transformation in *Hayavadana* points to Karnad's value system, which is basically humanistic, and his valuable solution to the problem of human identity crisis.

According to the folk drama convention, the image of Lord Ganesha has to be brought to the stage for offering a pooja to Him for the success of the play. After his pooja, the Bhagavata sings a song in praise of the God and pays obeisance to Him. Accepting Him as the omnipotent power, he notices the inherent contradiction, including identity crisis, within the God. Though He is the son of Lord Siva and Parvati, Lord Ganesha is incomplete and imperfect. For He has an elephantine head with a broken tusk and a cracked belly. Nevertheless, he is "the destroyer of incompleteness" (1). Significantly, He does not play any role in the lives of Karnad's protagonists, nor is played by any actor. He is presented as an external agency for ensuring the success of the play.

Second, among all the references that Hayavadana makes to the supernatural beings, his heavenly father is noticeable, though not acted by any character in the play. Hayavadana's father is a Celestial Being. Cursed by God Kubera, he comes to the *swayamvara* of the Princess of Karnataka, carrying the Prince of Araby. Strangely, he, who is in the form of a horse, is chosen by the Princess. He lives with her for fifteen years and then changes into his original shape. He leaves for Heaven turning his wife into a horse for disobedience. This is the first instance of a supernatural interaction with the humans in *Hayavadana* but proves to be unfavourable to the mortals.

Third, the Kali of Mount Chitrakoot, who is the "Mother of all Nature," appears in her own person as if to create identity crisis for the human beings. When Devadatta and Kapila reach her temple and cut off their head one after another separately, she is fast asleep but is aware of the happenings. Later when Padmini is about to offer her head, not only does the Goddess save her but also does she come forward to restore life to the dead bodies of Devadatta and Kapila. She instructs Padmini clearly about putting their heads and bodies together and placing the sword on their neck. Then she goes back to sleep never to wake up again. Of course, it is Padmini's mistake to mix-up the heads and bodies in her excitement. The Mother of all Nature, however, does not pay any heed to the helpless cries of Padmini to save her again. The Goddess's indifferent rather cruel atttitude is a clear case of divine malignity towards the human beings.

Fourth, Kali has her divine score against the human beings again when Hayavadana goes to her, seeking completion. Before he completes his prayer for complete man, the Goddess completes her sanction rather hastily and whimsically like the doctors who prescribe medicine before examining the patients thoroughly. Hayavadana becomes a complete horse much against his will but not a "complete being" since his human voice troubles him yet. Like Padmini, he too begs for Kali's mercy to make him a complete being. Silence and indifference are, however, the staple responses of the Goddess. Hayavadana seems to be aware of the fact that Kali is wilfully cruel. So he tells the Bhagavata: "The Goddess knew what she was doing. I can tell you that." (68) Here again, the Goddess's blessing turns out to be costly for Hayavadana.

All these four instances of the supernatural presence make it abundantly clear that Gods, Goddesses, and Celestial Beings have no real concern for desperate mortals on earth. Karnad seems to say, as the blinded Gloucester does in *King Lear*: "As flies to wanton boys are we to the Gods/ They kill us for their sport." True that Gloucester's view is partial but powerful enough to affect human beings.

Lord Ganesha does not interfere in the human affairs, neither positively nor negatively. The Celestial Being, who ought to have been grateful to Hayavadana's mother, turns savage to curse her. Perhaps the Celestial Beings too are not free from jealousy. Had the *gandharva* been magnanimous, he could have just left the Princess as a human being and transformed Hayavadana, his own son, into a complete man or complete horse, if not a divine being. Unfortunately, he has no good use for his divine power.

Unlike Lord Ganesha and the Celestial Being, Goddess Kali makes her presence felt directly. First, she is asleep. Next, she feels irritated by the capital sacrifices of her devotees like Padmini and Hayavadana. Then, she is insolent and reluctant to grant the prayers of her devotees. When she is roused from her sleep, she offers help half-heartedly. Such incomplete blessings add more woes to the incomplete beings. She does not really care to check whether or not the *bhaktas* are benefitted by and satisfied with her blessings.

Perhaps, if the Goddess had slept continuously without bothering about the visitors to her temple, they would not have been faced with more complicated problems. In fact, the identity crises of Padmini and Hayavadana become more critical after Kali's blessings. Had the Goddess remained quiet, Padmini would have died and her son would not have been born. Similarly, Hayavadana could have had his horse head and human body. Actually, he loves his mane so much that he "had to give the miss to Tirupati." (10) But then, Karnad could not have completed his Two-Act play. Thus it is seen that the supernatural beings play mischief with the protagonist (or does Karnad do that?) in *Hayavadana* and, indeed, cause the identity crisis.

From these rather unflattering presentations of the supernatural beings, it may be conjectured that Karnad is not a believer. His other plays like *Tughlaq, Naga-Mandala*, and *Tale-Danda* also provide sufficient evidence to this inference. In most of his interviews and discussions, he does not usually refer to his belief system. However, in his discussion with Anantha Murthy and Prasanna, he has admitted that he is an "atheist" (Murthy 1995: 128). Therefore, it is possible to suggest that the identity crisis caused by the external agents is rather unnecessary.

What then is the solution to the problem of human identity crisis? Obviously, Karnad does not accept the Indian idealistic solution, nor the German materialistic solution. He seems to favour a humanistic solution for which a clue can be found in his remark that "Not being happy with oneself is a mark of human existence" (Chakravartee 47). If unhappiness is the unalterable law of life, as Karnad appears to believe, it is good for the human beings, Karnad suggests, to accept the unhappy life happily instead of making it unhappier. Hence, Karnad adopts a pragmatic approach to end the play with *mangalam*, though "this comic effect is a bit ironic—rather tongue-in-cheek" (Raykar 342). Small wonder the Bhagavata's closing prayer to Lord Ganesha, composed by Karnad in 1970 remains, and is likely to remain, just a prayer. According to Karnad, it is better for the prayer to go unheeded because further problems may not arise. Then, the problem of identity crisis is not a crisis but a characteristic of the human beings with which they can live happily or otherwise as per their own choice. Realization comes to Padmini just before her death but Hayavadana has a hopeful future. Hayavadana's end is ridiculous, but then whose end is not so?

Girish Karnad's *Hayavadana*, thus, explores the complex psycho-social dimension of the problem of human identity crisis, as different from the moral aspect of the Indian story and the philosophical purport of Mann's story, in both tangled and untangled relationships. The play reveals the essential ambiguity of human personality which is apparently shaped or shattered by the human environment. Fundamentally incomplete and imperfect, the human beings search and strive for attaining the unattainable ideal of completeness and perfection. They usually tend to seek the assistance of some supernatural beings or the other to succeed in their endeavour. However, these external agencies, in their effort to help, seem to cause and complicate the identity crisis of the seekers further, leading the latter to tragic and/or comic ends. Padmini, for instance, ruins herself and all her relations. Even the child that she leaves under the Bhagavata's care is not normal because of her own compulsions. Hayavadana, for another instance, does not bring destruction to himself as Padmini does but suffers the drastic consequences of his search for completeness by going down the ladder of existence from man to horse. A close examination of Karnad's presentation of the supernatural beings, especially that of Kali, in *Hayavadana*, points to the playwright's atheistic leanings and suggests that they cannot help human beings unless the latter help themselves by accepting the psychological limitations imposed by nature. The best solution for the problem of identity crisis then, according to Girish Karnad, is reconciliation with one's own self and the environment.

The Romance of Influence: A Bloomian Perspective on *Hayavadana*

> Poets influence us because we fall in love with their poems. All love unfortunately changes, if indeed it does not end, and since nothing is got for nothing, we also get hurt when we abandon, or are abandoned by, poems. Criticism is as much a series of metaphors for the acts of loving what we have read as for the acts of reading themselves (Bloom 1976: 103).

A crucial criticism of theoretical importance against Harold Bloom is that his theory of anxiety of influence is difficult for others to practise. The criticism is largely justified as the passage of time shows. There are any number of Derridians, Lacanians, Focauldians, Bakhtinians, and so on but hardly a handful of Bloomians, as for example, Ann Wodsworth and Helen Regueiro Elam, though Bloom (1975: 88) has described his brand of criticism as "antithetical practical criticism" in direct contrast to the New Critical variety and the traditional method of influence study. Since Bloom's theory is not confined to individual texts and to direct borrowings from one author to another, it becomes extraordinarily difficult for his followers to have the founder's ingenuity and wide scholarship. However, Thais Morgan has shown how most intertextual theories, including Bloom's, are "conservative" only. (272)

Despite the difficulties with Harold Bloom, it appears

that a moderate application of his theory is possible, if taken seriously in his own spirit. As a test case on a small scale, Girish Karnad's *Hayavadana*, translated by the author from Kannada into English, has been chosen for three reasons. First, Karnad's play does not belong to Bloom's favourite field of the Western post-Romantic poetry, but to the Indian folk drama tradition. Next, the intertextual relation is not between poems as the usual case with Bloom, though he extended it to drama and novel later, but between a drama and a long short story. Lastly and importantly, the motif of poetic influence which is at the heart of Bloom's theory is dramatized by Karnad through Devadatta in conflict with Kalidasa, though it is incidental in *Hayavadana*. Naturally, the precursor text is "The Transposed Heads" by Thomas Mann (214-87) as acknowledged by Karnad (1985) in his "Note." Bloom may not accept this study of direct influence as Bloomian, but then Karnad has transformed the direct borrowing with Bloomian evasions.

When Karnad encountered the story of the transposed heads, he planned to film it. However, his friend B.V. Karanth suggested to him to write a play. Only then Karnad (1989a: 99) realized that the story was "actually theatrical." Again, he did not think of the play in terms of folk drama. The story by itself seemed to suggest to him that it would take the shape of a folk drama chiefly because of the change of heads, which could easily be managed on the stage with masks (Paul: 4). Gradually, all the other elements crept in: songs, dance, music, the Bhagavata, and so on. If Karnad had simply dramatized Mann's story, Bloom may not have any application here. But Karnad has introduced the motif of influence besides the secondary story of Hayavadana as a reflection on the main story of Devadatta, Kapila, and Padmini. That is why, the play offers a unique scope for appreciating Bloom's theory of influence and Karnad's creative anxiety. Then Karnad's double-plotting and influence motif can be studied with reference to Bloomian strategies of evasion.

The play deals with the story of Devadatta, Kapila, and Padmini, but it does not do so directly and immediately. The main story is interrupted and delayed until the first half of the story of Hayavadana is played out. Two important questions arise now. First, why is the main plot delayed? In his interview with Raykar, Karnad says that he "invented the story" because he had "always felt tremendous fascination for Shakespeare's sub-plots—how he tells the same story twice from two different points of view," and adds, "I have always aspired to write a sub-plot successfully." (341) Clearly then, Karnad has attempted to tell the story of the transposed heads through the story of the horse headed man. While Shakespeare can interweave the various plots in his plays, as many as four plots in *As You Like It*, Karnad has kept his two plots separate from each other except for the union of the Child and Hayavadana at the end. Even this half-hearted fusion of the two plots seems to be wrought with more problems than solutions. For example, how does one explain the transfer of human voice from Hayavadana to the child within the framework of the play? Further, the equine story gives the title to the play. Hayavadana is not the proper name of a person; it simply means the face of a horse. Is it the equine face of Karnad's imagination? Is there anything besides the playwright's sub-plot obsession that could substantiate the need for the Hayavadana plot?

It may, then, be posited that Mann's ridicule of the alleged supremacy of head over body is inadequate for Karnad. The horse head determining Hayavadana's complete being is, in fact, an extension of Mann's logic to its imagistically ridiculous end. How Hayavadana comes to have a horse head and human body is the core of the sub-plot, though Karnad does not try to provide any rational explanation. On the other hand, the playwright builds up a mythical story of Hayavadana's parentage.

The satirical edge is sharpened all the more, when it is revealed that Hayavadana's mother was the Princess of Karnataka and his father was a Celestial Being in the form of a horse due to a curse inflicted upon him by God Kubera. As a result of the unusual marriage of the Princess and the white stallion is born the hybrid child, Hayavadana. Neither the mother nor the father has any concern for the handicapped child who is left alone in the cruel world to search for his society. The father returns to his heavenly abode after fifteen years of marital life with the Princess. The mother is turned into a mare by none other than her own celestial husband, when he becomes irritated with her for her demand that he be a horse for her to accompany him to Heaven. While she joins the family of horses happily and the father his own society of *gandharvas*, the incongruous child has no place to live because he belongs nowhere, neither the *gandharvas*, nor the horses, not even the human beings. One finds more of sharp social satire in this equine story than in Mann who leaves the child Andhaka to become a great scholar. Karnad's double plotting of Mann's single plot, then, is a Bloomian revisionary stance. Consequently, the playwright's satirical supplement takes over Mann's philosophical complement to the original story of *Vetalapanchavimsati* in which King Vikram's verdict is accepted without question.

A caution is in order here. Bloom's categories of specific evasions, his six revisionary ratios with endless multiplications and modifications elaborated in book after book, are not used in this study. After all, as Bloom (1990-91: 200) has confessed, these exotic and quixotic terms are "meant to expose how arbitrarily all critical and rhetorical terminology always is and has to be." The proliferation of theories and counter theories in this century has proved Bloom's statement beyond doubt. As he says in another context, what matters is not the method but one's own self. To quote Bloom (1987: 67), "there is no method except yourself."

There is no doubt about the fact that Karnad has emerged as the strongest playwright in the scene of contemporary Indian drama. A major part of his strength lies in his ability to suffer and to overcome the poetic influence from various sources like the Sanskrit drama, the regional drama, the European drama, and the American drama. While Bloom bases his theory of anxiety of influence on the Freudian family romance, Karnad dramatizes the romance of poetic influence in his own play, in the main plot of *Hayavadana* which consists of a poet, a muse, and a poetic father to be conquered. Though the direction of the play changes drastically, the fact remains that the cause of the confusion of identities is poetic influence.

The ephebe, the young and growing poet in Karnad's play, is Devadatta. He is "the only son of the revered Brahmin Vidyasagara." (2) He has accomplished a lot of intellectual feats. He has won over the greatest pundits and poets. Though he is the unrivalled scholar and poet, he has the latent ambition of achieving victory over the masters of the past too. However, this ambition remains subdued until he sights Padmini one day. It is not that he has not been attracted to girls till now. In fact, as Kapila, his friend says, he has already "fallen in love fifteen times in the last two years." (12) What is unique about Padmini is that her sight brings out the creative anxiety in Devadatta to the fore and compels him to think about his inadequacies as a poet. As he says to Kapila, "I was blind all these days. I deceived myself that I understood poetry. I didn't. I understood nothing." (13) Kapila also confirms her uniqueness in an aside, "it does look as though this sixteenth girl has really caught our Devadatta in her net." (14) Padmini, thus, becomes the muse for igniting the fire of poetic influence in the ephebe Devadatta.

Based on the background and nature of Devadatta's love, it is possible to suggest that Padmini's *net* is the field of Bloom's romance of influence. Nothing else could be there in Padmini to make Devadatta to tell his friend, "Kapila in one appearance, she became my guru in the poetry of love. Do you think she would ever assent to becoming my disciple in love itself?" (14) The rhetorical question with a negative answer indicates that the ephebe has a defeatist attitude. As a matter of fact, the anguished Devadatta confesses, "What's the use? She isn't meant for the likes of me." (14) In this despairing mood, the head Devadatta loses his sense of reason. However, his friend Kapila, the body, takes the lead and volunteers to fulfill the head's desire.

If Devadatta is the ephebe and Padmini, the muse, the precursor poet is Kalidasa. In his unconscious anxiety to convince his friend about the importance of the muse, Devadatta tells Kapila, "If only she would consent to be *my Muse, I could outshine Kalidasa*. I'd always wanted to do that but I thought it was impossible. . . . But now it isn't all impossible" (14, emphasis added). Later, he identifies *Shakuntalam* as the chief literary text to be excelled. When Kapila replies that Devadatta should start writing poetry, the ephebe admits that he cannot write without possessing the muse. He adds that he cannot concentrate because his head and body are completely immersed in her.

It is the strong conviction of Devadatta that Padmini, the muse, would inspire him to achieve the almost impossible task of outshining Kalidasa that urges him to pray for his marriage with the muse. He offers to sacrifice his head to Lord Rudra and his hands to Goddess Kali, if ever he is able to marry Padmini and to have her as his wife. He feels himself lost and absolutely helpless just for the sake of a great literary ideal. He has the special poetic talent but is constrained for lack of an inspiring force. Though he has his close friend, Kapila cannot do anything about this extraordinary imaginative function. When the young poet realizes his predicament, he utters desperately, "What's the use of these hands and this head if I'm not to have her? My poetry won't live without her. *Shakuntalam* will never be excelled" (14). The problem is Devadatta himself cannot explain everything to Padmini about his urgent literary task. As he is in the grip of the influence of Kalidasa, he says that he has "no cloud for a messenger" and "no bee to show the way" (14). Kapila is supposed to be uneducated and unimaginative but he understands the peculiar mind of his friend. Then and there he becomes Kalidasa's cloud and bee to *contact* and *contract* Padmini for his friend. Thereafter, Devadatta's marriage with Padmini, the muse, ensues but unfortunately the course of events runs amuck. Up to this stage, however, the Bloomian perspective points to Karnad's own creative anxiety and his humanization of Kalidasa just like Coleridge's of Milton (Bloom 1974: 520).

Now the moot question is whether a man as a man can give up his life just for the sake of possessing a woman for a while. In Mann the love of Shridaman for Sita is physically romantic. He is attracted to her beauty and so falls in love with her. He too marries her with the help of his friend Nanda. There is no suggestion of the creative, literary and imaginative dimension in Shridaman's love and marriage with Sita. In contrast, Devadatta's love for Padmini in Karnad is creatively romantic. The young poet's inability to accept mortality as a poet compels him to wish for the temporary possession of the muse and to achieve poetic immortality. As Bloom (1975: 91) says, "no poet, as a poet, can wish to die, for that negates poethood." Then, Devadatta's wish for death—his sacrifice of head and hands—is a means for life, the eternal life guaranteed by outshining Kalidasa's *Shakuntalam*. Thus, the romance in Mann is purely Freudian and remains at the physical level whereas the romance in Karnad is partly Bloomian and raises to the creative level. Karnad's addition of the romance of influence is not a matter of an ordinary influence but an extraordinary Bloomian influence. Devadatta is perhaps a substitute for Karnad himself, for *Hayavadana* is in creative tension with *Shakuntalam* in the field of poetry as well as drama.

In a rare insightful observation on the poetic quality of the play, S. Gopalie (8) has remarked: "In *Hayavadana* we see a Karnad who Karnad himself did not discover before. Karnad the poet is more compelling than Karnad the playwright. But for sheer poetry of the theatre there is nothing that can challenge comparison with *Hayavadana*." Of all Karnad's plays, *Hayavadana* remains the most poetic and Gopalie's remark is valid until now. Possibly Karnad the failed poet entered into the characterization of Devadatta. In this context, it may be recalled that Karnad's early ambition was to become a famous poet in English. He spent his valuable years for learning English and mastering it to carve a niche for himself as an English poet. But when the opportunity came to him to go to the land of Auden and Eliot, he realized to his horror that the English people would read the English poets like Auden and Eliot only. As a result, he started writing his first play *Yayati* in Kannada even before reaching England. Karnad (1989: 85) expresses his anguish: "I wanted to be a poet: the greatest ambition in my life. At the age of 22, I realized I would not become a poet, but only be a playwright, then I almost wept." Obviously the frustrated poet in Karnad found his manifestation in Devadatta. Karnad has miraculously survived but his alter ego Devadatta commits suicide at the Kali temple saying that he sacrifices himself in gratitude. Painfully he discovers that his muse Padmini has deserted him for the sake of his friend Kapila. Owing to the complications of personal relations, Devadatta forgets his poetic relations with Kalidāsa. There are no signs of his ever attempting to think about his poetic rival after his marriage. Unfortunately, the poet, the muse, and the friend all die but Kalidasa lives on within and outside *Hayavadana*.

What, then, are the critical lessons that can be learnt from the episode of influence in Karnad's *Hayavadana* by the Bloomian readers? The following salient lessons may be noted down here, though many more subtle lessons of both theoretical and practical significance could be derived. First, an ambitious ephebe like Devadatta needs the muse to compete with the greatest precursors like Kalidasa. Second, the muse may be coquettish. Third, the young poet has to exert a tremendous control over the muse for achieving his goal, or else he may be ruined even before he begins his attempt. Fourth, Bloom's theory of poetic influence illuminates Karnad's practice of dramatic influence and vice-versa. The tragic end in both Bloom and Karnad is the inevitable result of all Gnostic enterprise, as Bloom has repeatedly shown, especially in his adventurous fiction (Bloom 1979) and as Karnad has often revealed, particularly in *Hayavadana*. Here ends the romance of influence in relation to Bloom and Karnad, and begins the anxiety of influence with reference to the critic and his readers.

The Literary Genetics of *Hayavadana*

In his "Note" to *Hayavadana* Girish Karnad states unambiguously that "the central episode in the play—the story of Devadatta and Kapila is based on a tale from the *Kathasaritsagara* but I have heavily drawn on Thomas Mann's reworking of the tale in "The Transposed Heads" and am grateful to Mrs. Mann for permission to do so" (Karnad 1985). More or less Karnad's statement is true since he has followed Mann faithfully to a large extent as far as the main plot of *Hayavadana* is concerned, though he has effected his own creative additions, deletions and transmutations. Shridhar B. Shrotri and Majan M. Mulla (1975-76), M.K. Naik (1984) and others have studied the traditional aspects of influence between Mann and Karnad. None of them, however, explains satisfactorily why the play is titled *Hayavadana.* To solve this problem, an attempt is made here to study the literary genetics of the play beyond Mann to Kalidasa's *Shakuntala* and the episode of Shakuntala in Vyasa's the *Mahabharata*. It is suspected that Karnad owes more to Vyasa and Kalidasa than to Mann as he has ingeniously double plotted the romantic story of Shakuntala into the anti-romantic stories of Padmini and Hayavadana.

Girish Karnad is no stranger to the world of Indian myths, including the epics and puranas. As his contemporary playwright Vijay Tendulkar puts it aptly, Karnad was "groomed in mythology" (Ramnarayan 1998: 15). Karnad too has admitted on more than one occasion that he grew up with "a lot of myths" (see, for instance, Chakravartee 48). It is not surprising then that his very first play *Yayati* is based on *Adiparva,* the first book of the *Mahabharata.* Interestingly, the story of Shakuntala is also from the same book *Adiparva.* Like his illustrious and immortal predecessors Kalidasa and Shakespeare, Karnad has mostly adapted his plots from various sources. Like them again, he has endowed his borrowed stories with a new lease of life by adding his own share of myths. Chitralekha in *Yayati* and Hayavadana in *Hayavadana* are good examples of his myth-making imagination.

The relation of *Yayati* with the *Mahabharata* is direct and obvious, for the whole play deals with the original episode centring around Yayati. But the relation of *Hayavadana* with the *Mahabharata* is not so, for this play is chiefly shaped out of Thomas Mann's "The Transposed Heads." Nevertheless, the episode of poetic influence (Dhanavel 1993: 118-20) that Karnad has superimposed on Mann's story offers a sound basis for the incontestable analogy between Shakuntala, Dushyanta, and the bee of Kalidasa on the one hand, and Padmini, Devadatta and Kapila of Karnad on the other, of course, via Sita, Shridaman and Nanda of Mann. Though the analogical episode lasts for a few minutes only, about a page in the text, the whole play takes on the Kalidasa and Vyasa colour when its literary genetics is explored beyond Mann.

If the first extension to Kalidasa suggests that Padmini is Shakuntala, the second extension to Vyasa points to the fact that Karnad's invented character Hayavadana is after all a dexterous transmutation of Shakuntala. This literary genetic framework of tridadic relationship among Karnad, Kalidasa, and Vyasa further indicates that the theme of *Hayavadana* is not so much of "the mad dance of incompleteness" (Karnad 1985: 57) as that of the plight of abandoned children in an indifferent world. Moreover, this framework explains why Karnad chose to title the play *Hayavadana* without any reference to "the central episode of Devadatta and Kapila." Above all, it throws light on the deeper original, genealogical and historical concerns of Karnad about contemporary free India—Bharat—Hayavadana, Padmini, and the morose child.

Vyasa has created the prototype of Shakuntala in the first book of the *Mahabharata* which records the genealogy of the Pandavas and the Kauravas as well as accounts for Bharata, the son of Shakuntala and Dushyanta. As well known, Shakuntala is the daughter of the great sage Vishwamitra and the celestial nymph Menaka. When the sage does not want to look after the baby, the nymph does not like to take her along to heaven. Consequently, the innocent baby is left on the banks of the river Malini. Fortunately, she is protected by the birds around and that is why she is called Shakuntala. Later, another sage called Kanva brings her up to be a beautiful maiden.

It so happens that Dushyanta, the king of Hastinapur, reaches Kanva's ashram while on a hunting expedition. Desiring to pay homage to the rishi, he visits the ashram only to be welcomed by Shakuntala since her foster-father is temporarily away collecting flowers for worship. Passionate love at first sight compels Dushyanta to negotiate with her for marriage. On condition of her son being declared heir to the throne, she agrees to marry him according to the *gandharva* rites. After consummating his marriage, Dushyanta leaves for the palace hoping to send a royal team for taking Shakuntala there, though he fails to keep his word for long.

On his return Kanva learns of the consummated marriage

and looks after Shakuntala patiently and carefully. She gives birth to a brilliant boy who grows up to be uncontrollably mischievous. It is then Kanva decides to send Shakuntala and her son to Dushyanta so that the boy could rightfully be declared the prince. But the king pretends to have no remembrance of his marriage to Shakuntala. When all her attempts to revive the king's memory fail, she deplores her condition feelingly: "What wrong had I done that I was abandoned by my parents and why am I now being disowned by my husband?" (Khosla 9). At this juncture, a voice from heaven bears testimony to Shakuntala. Thereafter, the king accepts her as his chief queen and his son as heir-apparent. It is this son Sarvadaman who is known as Bharata after whom the country is called Bharat.

Vyasa's artless story of genealogical importance becomes a sylvan, rather golden, story of poetic and dramatic importance, not only in the Indian context but also in the global context. Ever since Georg Forster's German translation appeared in 1781 and William Jones's English translation in 1789, Kalidasa's *Shakuntala* has come to be regarded as an immortal world drama, though the Western mind has found it difficult to accept the Indian ethos embedded in the play.

Kalidasa took the bare skeleton of the story from Vyasa but infused it with an unparallelled imaginative power. Like an architectural genius, he has built the play into a wonderful monument of love. Kalidasa's Dushyanta is drawn into Kanva's hermitage by the fearful deer and then led to Shakuntala by the fearful bee. Priyamvada and Anasuya, Shakuntala's companions, play a significant role in the *gandharva* marriage of Dushyanta and Shakuntala. While Kanva is sent on a piligrimage, Durvasa is introduced to utter a near fatal curse on Shakuntala. This episode naturally fits in with that of the ring. Kanva sends his daughter to Dushyanta as soon as he hears of the marriage. While the king's blameless character is glorified, Menaka's motherly concern is highlighted as she carries off Shakuntala to Kashyapa's ashram. The lost ring is found dramatically to cause repentance in Dushyanta whose intense sufferings are observed by the invisible Sanumati, a friend of Shakuntala. The King of Gods, Indra, invites Dushyanta to heaven for waging a war against the disturbing demons and then enables him to reunite with his wife and son at Kashyapa's ashram.

Even the compassionate and large-hearted Kalidasa could not but give vent to Shakuntala's innermost feelings of abandonment and desolation, when rejected by the king, this time not out of pretension but out of forgetfulness, the inevitable effect of Durvasa's curse. When Saradwata, a sanyasi who is also a member of the escort of Shakuntala, finally decides to leave her with the king and go to Kanva's ashram, Shakuntala bursts out in tears: "What! Is it not enough to have been betrayed by this perfidious man? Must you also forsake me regardless of my tears and lamentations?" (205)

Vyasa and Kalidasa are unanimous in their presentation of Shakuntala as an abandoned person, child, girl, wife, and mother. Vyasa gives immediate relief to Shakuntala but Kalidasa takes a long time to work out the dramatic reunion of Shakuntala with her husband at Kashyapa's ashram. By that time, she is completely emaciated and found in a widow's dress. If Vyasa's concerns regarding Shakuntala are mainly genealogical, Kalidasa's interests are primarily dramatic. Their plots do not have any scope for investigation into the psychological depths of Shakuntala's sufferings as a child deserted by her parents, though both of them are equally prominent in their respective realms, as a rejected wife, that too with a child grown up in Vyasa and conceived in Kalidasa, by her own husband who is none other than the King of Hastinapur. It is this forsaken person who draws the attention of Girish Karnad in *Hayavadana*.

Obviously Padmini, "the daughter of the leading merchant in Dharmapura" (Karnad 1985: 19) with whom Devadatta, "comely in appearance, fair in colour, unrivalled in intelligence," (2) falls in love, is Karnad's Shakuntala. There are a few references in the play which emphasize this view. In the words of Devadatta, Padmini is "the Shyama Nayika born of Kalidasa's magic description—as Vatsyayana had dreamt her." (13-14) On seeing Padmini face-to-face, Kapila expresses his appreciation of her in an aside: "I give up, Devadatta. I surrender to your judgement. I hadn't thought anyone could be more beautiful than the wench Ragini who acts Rambha in our village troupe. But this one! You're right—she is Yakshini, Shakuntala, Urvashi, Indumati—all rolled into one." (16) Of all the beauties referred to by Kapila, Shakuntala stands out among them for her beauty, gaiety, modesty, and many other desirable qualities.

The references of Devadatta and Kapila are not just to Shakuntala as a character alone. Actually, the whole context of Kalidasa's play is brought in. For instance, Devadatta is aggrieved that "I have no cloud for a messenger. Nobody to show the way." (14) But Kapila, his dearest friend, offers to be the cloud-messenger, bee, and pigeon, and acts upon his words at once. The allusion to Dushyanta being led first by a deer and then by a bee to Shakuntala is apparent. As such Devadatta is Karnad's Dushyanta and Kapila his bee. Moreover, the association of Shakuntala and birds is suggested by the door-frame of Padmini's house, which has "an engraving of a two-headed bird at the top." (15) In fact, it is by this mark that Kapila is able to identify her house. One more notable connection is that of lotus. Kalidasa's

Shakuntala writes her love letter on a lotus leaf for Dushyanta, and Karnad's Padmini is lotus itself as her name implies. All these references testify that Padmini is Karnad's Shakuntala.

In Kalidasa, the motifs of love, marriage, separation, and union combine together to make the play. In Karnad, the motifs of love and marriage come in more for poetic reasons than political. Further, the conflict in Karnad arises from Padmini herself. Though she marries Devadatta, she starts drifting towards Kapila. This conflict is dramatically presented through the transposition of heads at the Kali temple. Before and after the transposition, Padmini is found herself alone completely neglected by both her husband and her 'lover.' First Devadatta dies and then Kapila follows suit without ever thinking about Padmini. After their revival, Devadatta pursues his studies and Kapila goes into the forest. Again she is disregarded by both when they fight with each other and kill themselves. Circumstantially, Padmini is forced to enter fire but the mother in her tells the Bhagavata to take care of her child. Analyzing the whole situation, Padmini remarks sadly, "You forgave each other, but again left me out." (62) The romantic story of Shakuntala is thus transfigured in the anti-romantic story of Padmini.

Neither does Karnad glorify the love of Devadatta, Padmini, and Kapila, nor does he idealize the friendship of Devadatta and Kapila. He aims at presenting the conflicts and consequences attendant upon divided love with adequate psychological realism and personal symbolism. However, it seems that the psychological tensions of a woman in love with two men are not so significant dramatically as to be reflected in the title of the play. That is where the hidden trajectory of genetic relationship between Shakuntala and Hayavadana needs to be examined in detail.

The sub-plot of Hayavadana is generally seen in relation to the main plot of Devadatta, Kapila, and Padmini as a deeper reflection of the same theme of incompleteness at the animal level. In fact, Karnad "invented the story for the same obsession with sub-plot that I have always had" (Raykar 1982: 341). He had an earnest desire to write plays with double plots as Shakespeare did successfully in *Hamlet, King Lear* and many other plays. But neither his obsession with sub-plot, nor his interest in the theme of incompleteness accounts for the reversed roles of main plot and sub-plot. As per the Shakespearean plays or Jonsonian, or Congrevian, or Sheridanian, or Wildean, or even Shavian plays, the sub-plot should have been subsumed under the main plot. But Karnad envelopes the main plot within the sub-plot in the title of the play. Perhaps Karnad attempts to subvert this dramatic convention but to what end?

A close reading of Vyasa, Kalidasa, and Karnad suggests that Karnad has very subtly transformed the archetypal Shakuntala into Hayavadana. Given his propensity for transformational tactics, the case of Hayavadana is nothing unusual. Yet it is unusual and surprising because he plays tricks with the gender (identity) of his character—from woman to man to horse. The Bhagavata's confusion about Hayavadana sums up the identity crisis appropriately "Him? It? What's coming?" (5) Prior to these two pronouns can be added "Her?"

There are quite a few similarities between the life of Shakuntala and Hayavadana. While Shakuntala is the daughter of a great rishi and a celestial nymph, Hayavadana is the "son" of a great princess and a celestial being. Both the parents of Shakuntala abandon her to be looked after first by birds and then by Kanva. Similarly, both the parents of Hayavadana forsake him. His celestial father returns to heaven and his mother, cursed by her husband to become a horse, joins the horse family. Hayavadana is partly a celestial being, partly a human being, and partly an animal being. But he cries with anguish about his desertion. He says to the Bhagavata: "Only I—the child of their marriage was left behind." (9) Further, he asks the Bhagavata, "But where's my society? Where? You must help me to become a complete man, Bhagavata Sir. But how? What can I do?" (9) These bemoaning words of Hayavadana directly bring to mind Vyasa's Shakuntala.

The misfortune of Hayavadana is more pathetic than that of Shakuntala because he is neither a complete human being nor a complete horse. He also does not have birds nor a kind step-father like Kanva to look after him. His future is bleak and he has nothing to do except search for his completeness. He visits all prominent holy places and persons but his desire for completeness remains unfulfilled. When Goddess Kali grants his wish without listening to him fully, he is aghast to find himself a complete horse. Still he is bothered by the human voice. In this condition he happens to meet Padmini's son for whom he laughs and loses his voice resulting in proper neigh.

The plight of Hayavadana may represent the human condition of mock existence in a world of irresponsible parents. In the existentialist framework such a view may be valid. In fact, several critics have noted the existential dimension of the play with approval. However, it is really difficult for a person groomed in Indian mythology to embrace the absurd philosophy. Indeed, Karnad has confessed that he could respond to Beckett's plays like *Waiting for Godot* and *No Exit* but not write one (Ramnarayan 14).

Therefore, it is argued that Karnad has double plotted the romantic story of Shakuntala into the anti-romantic stories of Padmini and Hayavadana. Since he has been able to narrate the story of Hayavadana much more meaningfully and dramatically than that of Padmini, he has ventured to title his play *Hayavadana*. Otherwise there is no reason why he should not have called his play *Padmini* or *Devadatta and Kapila*, or *The Transposed Heads* or even *Dance of Incompleteness*. Despite the fact that Karnad has admitted his heavy debt to Mann, it is clearly seen that he owes more to Vyasa and Kalidasa not only for the characterization of Padmini but also for Hayavadana. Further, it is suggested that the theme of the play pivots on the question of abandoned children and not so much on the search for completeness. Even the reference to the elephant-headed God is a sly attack on Lord Siva and Lady Parvati. Thus the literary genetics of Girish Karnad's *Hayavadana* finally brings out the subtle aspects of Karnad's art of appropriation and science of synergization.

Hayavadana: A Study in Condensation

The dramatic world of Girish Karnad's *Hayavadana* is "bizarre" (Kurtkoti 1985: vi) and "topsy-turvy" (Freud 1966:180). But it is not unreal as it presents the reality of man's everyday dreams. In fact, the whole play can be considered a manifest dream with a latent content. Therefore, a psychoanalytic study of the play with reference to the defense mechanism of condensation may be helpful in understanding some of the critical problems raised by the play.

As a critical necessity, then, a brief account of condensation is in order. Condensation is one of the major defence mechanisms employed by the Id in the dream process to allow the undesirable wishes to appear in the dream in distorted forms. To quote Freud, "by that [condensation] we understand the fact that the manifest dream has a smaller content than the latent one, and is thus an abbreviated translation of it." (1966:171) It is present in all dreams and does not occur in its reverse form, that is, the latent content is never smaller than the manifest dream. What happens in the condensation process is that two or more than two elements are fused together to make a single unity which is seen in the actual dream.

Illustrations for the oneiric activity are plenty in world mythology, literature, arts, and many other areas. However, the mythological instances are immediately appealing and attractive. For example, centaur is of half man and half horse, minotaur is of half man and half bull, and sphinx is of a lion's body and a woman's head. The three witches in Shakespeare's *Macbeth* and Hayavadana in Karnad's *Hayavadana* are good literary examples. Condensation can also be seen in word formation for which examples include common words like dorse—donkey and horse, and brunch—break fast and lunch. This combination of different elements, a metaphorical process par excellence, is the basis of any creative activity, says Freud. (1966:172)

Girish Karnad is well-known for the condensational and transformational dramatic strategies in his plays (see Paranjape, 82-91). In *Hayavadana*, condensation operates at various levels. At the technical and formal level, the image of Lord Ganesha, a *Yakshagana* requirement for the ritualistic purpose, is a combination of three orders of experience: the divine, the human, and the animal. Similarly, *Hayavadana*, the eponymous character of the play, is an amalgamation of both the human and the animal orders. The actual condensation takes place on the stage with the transposition of heads between Devadatta and Kapila, which results in the emergence of a perfect man, Devadatta's head and Kapila's body, for a short duration. A similar interchange, not of body but of voice and silence, occurs between *Hayavadana* and the child. Besides, there are subtle fusions of themes, structures, and genres in the play, which warrant a close study for an appreciation of Karnad's condensational dramatic art.

It is merely a technical feature of a *Yakshagana* play to have the image of Lord Ganesha and perform a pooja for Him for the success of the play. Karnad, however, seems to have realized the rich thematic connotations of the image through the poetic and prose rendering of the Bhagavata's prayer which is highly suggestive of the playwright's chief concern throughout the play. Lord Ganesha, representing a perfect blend of three different worlds of experience—the divine, the human, and the animal—is the "destroyer of incompleteness." (1) Simultaneously, He is the "embodiment of imperfection, of incompleteness" as well as "the Lord Master of Success and Perfection." (1) Interestingly, the concluding part of the Bhagavata's invocation to this paradoxical god resonates with a sense of mystery: "It is not for us to understand this Mystery or try to unravel it. Nor is it within our powers to do so. Our duty is merely to pay homage to the Elephant-headed god and get on with our play." (1)

In a very important sense Lord Ganesha "pervades" (Mukherjee 137) the whole play. He foreshadows the character of *Hayavadana* and is a contrast to Goddess Kali whose role is played by an actor on the stage. Significantly, the Bhagavata does not direct *Hayavadana* to Lord Ganesha for the destruction of his incompleteness but to the goddess. None of the characters mentions Him in the play. But at the end, the Bhagavata thanks the Mangalamoorthy for His grace in fulfilling the desires of a grandfather, a child, and a horse. Then; joining all the other actors, he also prays to Lord Ganesha:

> Grant us, O Lord, good rains, good crop,
> Prosperity in poetry, science, industry, and other affairs,
> Give the rulers of our country success in all endeavours,
> and along with it, a little bit of sense. (71)

Thus worshipped, the God's mystery of incompleteness and imperfection is accepted without question whereas other gods, goddesses, saints, and rishis are ridiculed along with the incomplete characters.

Intitially a man with the face of a horse, Hayavadana

is the titular protagonist of the play, though he appears in the sub-plot. His accidental appearance on the stage is, in fact, an interruption of the main story. As a result, he annoys the Bhagavata, who is staging the drama of the transposed heads. However, the plight of Hayavadana evokes sympathy in the heart of the Bhagavata who listens to his tragic story attentively. Then, he is directed by the Bhagavata to go to Goddess Kali at Mount Chitrakoot for his desire for completeness to be fulfilled. Strangely, neither Hayavadana nor the Bhagavata mentions Lord Ganesha.

In contrast to Lord Ganesha, Hayavadana is a live example of condensation. He has a human body on an equine head. He speaks eloquently and puts forward his case of incompleteness very impressively. It seems that the main problem posed by Karnad through Hayavadana is not simply how to achieve completeness. The problem is concerned with a dramatic exploration of the rationale of discordant birth and existence: Why was Hayavadana born like this? Who is responsible for his incongruous condition?

When Hayavadana says, "Only I—the child of their marriage—was left behind," (9) there is a sort of intense repulsion about his parents. His celestial father had left for Heaven and his earthly mother, turned into a mare by her husband's curse on her demand for him to remain a horse, joined the equine family. The 'child' Hayavadana is left alone on the earth to search for his society. He has everything of the human race in him except the equine face. This combination of a man's body and a horse's head does not allow him to be a member of either category. Hence, he asks the Bhagavata: "But where is my society? Where? You must help me to become a complete man, Bhagavata Sir. But how? What can I do?" (9) The Bhagavata, however, is unable to answer him satisfactorily, not even with his theory of karma.

Again, Hayavadana intervenes in the main play when it is about to end. Surprisingly, he appears as a complete horse with the blessings of the Goddess, though the human voice remains with him. Now his trouble is how to remove it. This time he does not have to go to any god or goddess. He just laughs to amuse Padmini's child and loses his voice to get his proper neigh. Thus he becomes a complete horse and a complete being, when the operation of condensation stops.

The most interesting condensation takes place on the stage when Padmini transposes the heads of Devadatta and Kapila. The whole frenzied action of Padmini at the temple of Goddess Kali is presented as if it happens accidentally. Some critics have noted the possible Freudian slip in this case (as for example, Mukherjee 134). Actually, it is a Freudian slip. Padmini's desire is that she should have a complete and perfect man for her husband. But neither Devadatta, nor Kapila is perfect individually because each represents one aspect only. When the opportunity presents itself before her for the joining of heads and bodies together, their transposition occurs quite naturally. As in a dream, the wish is fulfilled. In reality, however, every desire is a transgression of the law. When Padmini realizes her mistake, it is too late.

As Devadatta and Kapila rise in their changed form, they are not aware of their transposition. When Padmini cries in confusion, the friends, however, sing in joy about the exchanged heads. In fact, they thank her for this miraculous happening:

Devadatta: How fantastic! All these years we were only friends.
Kapila: Now we are blood-relations! Body-relations [laughing] what a gift!
Devadatta: Forgive you? We must thank you . . .
Kapila: We'll never be able to thank you enough . . . (35)

This dialogue of Devadatta and Kapila reveals that they had rather unconsciously wanted to become one in physique also Therefore, the desire of both Devadatta and Kapila on the one hand and the desire of Padmini on the other are one and the same for a perfect man, which is possible only through a combination of many good elements.

The cause of the transposition can thus be located in the desire of Padmini. To understand her inner mind, the song of the female chorus, which is sung both at the beginning and at the end of the play may be discussed.

> Why should love stick to the sap of a single body? When the stem is drunk with the thick yearning of the many-petalled, many-flowered lantana, why should it be tied down to the relation of a single flower? (11)

The single stem of Padmini is endowed with the treasure of many petals and many flowers. When the natural image of the single stem and many flowers is applied to the social image of marriage and family, there is discordance and discontentment. In this way monogamy is questioned by the play.

It is true that Devadatta and Kapila wanted to become one in their person. Their dream of unity in one person has the desire of having one wife also. Just before the sword fight, both of them express their love for Padmini without any hesitation. When Kapila proposes that they could "all live together—like the Pandavas and Draupadi," (60) Devadatta considers the idea seriously. But Padmini is unable to say anything positively. Contradiction can be smoothed over in condensation but not in reality. All the three realize their difficulties and adopt the course of suicide.

The main plot, then, is chiefly concerned with the social and psychological problem of a woman living with more than one husband, in addition to the problem of the future of children born of such relationships, as Karnad himself has pointed out in an interview (Raykar 342). In theme and treatment, *Hayavadana* is close to Anton Chekhov's short story "Ninochka: A Love Story" where the pale husband Vikhlyenev confronts the truth that his wife Ninochka loves his friend. Of course, Chekhov is a Russian and Karnad an Indian.

A different kind of condensation relates Hayavadana with the Child. The immediate bond between them is their plight as abandoned children in the world of selfish and indifferent parents. Though the nameless child is complete in all respects, he is an abnormal child. He is morose and easily irritable; he does not ask questions like Hayavadana; he cannot allow others to touch his dolls. Probably, the dramatist leaves the audience with some moral and social questions: first, why do parents beget children? and next, why do they neglect their own children?

It is possible that Karnad wants his audience to shed off the romantic notions they have about marriage, children and life. At one point, Hayavadana doubts the Bhagavata's theory of the child's pure laughter. He says: "it's this sort of sentimentality which has been the bane of our literature and national life. It has kept us from accepting Reality and encouraged escapism." (70) Significantly, Hayavadana loses his power of speech and gains his neigh just after this remark, as though the speech of Hayavadana had transferred to the child. This transposition of human voice is a wonderful work of condensation in the play.

Karnad has condensed several themes in this play to make it rich in its literary and cultural importance. The themes of identity, incompleteness, love (Sharma 1978:69-73), poetic influence (Dhanavel 1993: 118-20), mind-body dichotomy, theatre, social system and so on have been effectively brought together by Karnad. The whole play progresses like an underground river which springs out in several places in different directions and yet remains a forceful and vigorous river reaching out to the sea of human experiences. It is not without significance that Karnad has introduced the river symbolism in the play. While the *Mahabharata* glorifies polyandry, *Hayavadana* acknowledges the psychological reality of polyandry and its social rejection.

Structurally, the play has three major frames: the main plot, the sub-plot, and the folk-form. G.H. Nayak (1973: 93-113) has pointed out the incompleteness of the two plots and the necessity of combining them together to make the play complete. In addition, it may be observed that the two plots have been encased in the folk form which is again a masterly combination of the Oriental and Western dramatic elements with an emphasis on the precarious distance between high and low art forms. The play acting of the Bhagavata and his troupe itself is a play; it is a sort of superframe. All these three frames are necessarily incomplete as they embody the theme of incompleteness.

For a better understanding of the three interdependent dramatic frames, a diagrammatic picture is given below:

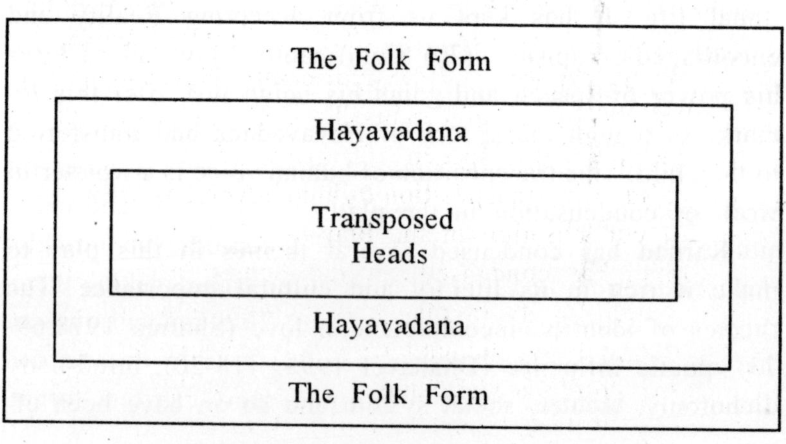

Thus, the main plot of the transposed heads is enshrined at the centre of the play around which are built the inner wall of the sub-plot and then the precincts of the folk form. Lord Ganesha remains the entry as well as the exit point for the play. Evidently, Karnad's approach to drama is religious and reverential, though his plays are generally concerned with irreligion and irreverence.

If the major theme of the play is incompleteness, it may be held that the entire play is incomplete both structurally and thematically. Metaphysically it may be argued that man is incomplete and so whatever he creates is bound to fall short of completion. Very interestingly, the fragmentary nature of the play calls for a consideration of a postmodern reading. Though Karnad has tried to make it unified, the play shows its incoherences at several points. The *mangalam* of the play, then, is only an imposition of the dramatist.

In Karnad's own admission (Raykar 342), *Hayavadana* is a comedy with a tragedy behind it. But it is not a tragicomedy like Shakespeare's *Measure for Measure*, nor *The Merchant of Venice*, nor *The Winter's Tale*. As Murthy (1976: 37) has remarked, the play has a serious theme but treats it comically leading to the problem of "relevance of audience response." The main plot of Devadatta, Kapila, and Padmini is really tragic when they die at the end. The sub-plot of *Hayavadana* is also equally pathetic. But the play ends with a note of joy and laughter. The whole play also permeates with a peculiar sense of humour which is of the order of Shakespeare's *Antony and Cleopatra* in its variety and magnitude. Since Karnad planned it as a comedy, he brought Hayavadana and the Child together at the close, making them laugh and with them the audience too. This condensation at the generic level has become possible mainly due to the Chaucerian humane vision of Karnad. How can one forget the Miller's tale of Joseph, the scholar, while reading *Hayavadana*?

Freud's condensation is, thus, helpful in understandinag the bizarre world of Karnad's *Hayavadana*. The play's manifest content reveals the operation of condensation at various levels: the image of Lord Ganesha, Hayavadana, the transposition of heads, the interchange of speech and silence, theme, structure, and genre. The defence mechanism of condensation shows an essential aspect of Karnad's creative genius in his presentation of a probable dreamy world to a scientifically advanced urban audience, drawing its attention to the consequences of frustrated desires of the decentred modern self.

The Desire for Recognition: A Lacanian Reading of *Hayavadana*

Of the four plays of Girish Karnad, translated into English by himself, *Tughlaq* and *Tale-Danda* are historical, and *Hayavadana* and *Naga-Mandala* are mythical. Strikingly, the historical plays explore two great men and the mythical plays examine two ordinary women. Though each of them is unique in its achievements, *Hayavadana* stands out as an incomparable play of incompleteness and identity crisis. While *Hayavadana* embodies the theme in his physical appearance of equine head and anthropic body, Devadatta and Kapila enact the theme in the transformation of their heads. Padmini, on the other hand, illustrates the psychological and philosophical lack in her through her quest for a complete man. All these characters suffer from the ontological problems of "fate," "desire," and "lack" which are at the root of Lacanian psychoanalysis. Therefore, an attempt is made to bring out the signifying chain of desire in *Hayavadana* through a Lacanian reading.

Jacques Lacan is one of the triple pillars of the influential poststructuralist movement, the other two being Jacques Derrida and Michel Foucault. If Derrida draws on Edmund Husserl and Martin Heidegger for his deconstructive enterprise, and if Foucault relies on Friedrich Nietzsche for his genealogical exploration, Lacan falls back on Sigmund Freud for his psychoanalytic reconnaissance. Among other sources, all the three have employed Ferdenand de Saussure in different ways to achieve their post-Saussurean and post-structuralist ends.

In his celebrated "return to Freud," Lacan has used not only the tools of Saussure but also those of Claude Levi-Strauss, Roman Jakobson, Gottlieb Frege, and many other thinkers. The result is not surprisingly the re-discovery of a Freud who is more a linguist and literary critic than a psychoanalyst. For Freud highlighted language as the bedrock of psychoanalysis in his early model of conscious, preconscious, and unconscious mind. Talking cure, interpretation of dreams, slips of the tongue and pen, and the whole interaction between the analyst and the analysand are all done with and through language. It is this linguistic Freud who is dear to Lacan and his French psychoanalysis. In fact, Lacan has faulted Freud and his followers, especially the American ego psychologists like Eric Fromm and Karen Horney, for deviating from the original discovery of the linguistic structure of the unconscious in favour of the scientific model of Id, Ego, and Superego which is accepted by the International Psychoanalytic Association.

What Lacan has done, then, is to read Freud closely and reinterpret him in the light of discoveries in the linguistic sciences. Accordingly, he has re-defined the Unconscious which, for him, is "neither primordial nor instinctual. what it knows about the elementary is no more than the elements of the signifier" (Lacan 1972:316). In his well-known statement, "the Unconscious is structured like a language." He has, indeed, argued impressively that it is language that creates the Unconscious when the child enters the language phase. Further, he has added that it is language that speaks and writes man, not the other way round (Lacan 1968: 201-2).

Lacan considers the human being as a subject "in order

to avoid connotations of selfhood and personhood" (Wright 107). In sharp contrast to the ego psychologists, he denies ego, selfhood, personality, individuality and similar notions which imply that man is a whole and unified entity. First, the unified and coherent ego is a product of the crucial misrecognition in the child's mirror stage when he can recognize his own image in the mirror. Next, the child is subjected to the tyranny of language which breaks into him for creating division rather than unity within him. Therefore, the child becomes a subject, a human subject, to be precise, because of his fragmented nature, and so, a divided subject with a strong desire for wholeness and recognition.

The child is born in an amorphous, fragmented, and undifferentiated state. He is not even able to recognize his own body as different from his mother's. Indeed, he mistakes his mother's body as his own. In this pre-mirror stage, he is just receptive to pain and pleasure. It is in the mirror stage from the sixth month to the eighteenth month that the child begins to recognize his image in the mirror. The reflected image is only a shadow, an *imago*, but the child misrecognizes it to be his total self and finds pleasure in the image. The child's initial identification with the mirrored image is known as "primary identification." It is "the basis of all subsequent secondary identification" (Muller and Richardson 1982: 30) throughout his life. This identification with images belongs to the Imaginary Order in Lacan's scheme.

During the pre-mirror and mirror stages, the child and the mother have a complementary relationship. As the child depends on the mother for nourishment and warmth, so does the mother depend on him for her fulfilment, the fulfilment of a fundamental lack in her, that is, phallus. Notably, Lacan divests phallus of its lexical meaning and attributes a symbolic meaning of power. Both the mother and the child are happy with each other in this symbiotic relationship. Importantly, the child does not experience any kind of repression and so the Unconscious is unknown to him.

The blissful and harmonious relationship between the mother and the child is threatened with the entry of the father, who is the representative of society, language, culture and so on. To refer to the symbolic nature of the father, who need not necessarily be the biological one, Lacan uses the phrase "Name-of-the-Father" or "Law-of-the-Father." The law is that of familial and matrimonial codes. The child's wish to possess the mother, then, is naturally repressed and pushed down to the Unconscious. The child is given a name and routed through the pre-established roles. To become a normal child, he has to accept the assigned roles. Interestingly, the arrival of the father, learning of language, and creation of the Unconscious all take place simultaneously. Hence, it is called the Oedipal stage as well as the linguistic stage. Now the child enters the Symbolic Order in which he learns the rules of social living.

If the Imaginary Order is a world of images, the Symbolic Order is a domain of taboos. The subject has to follow the rules and regulations of the society to fulfil his wishes. Otherwise, he will be punished. With this discipline of desires, the subject becomes all the more divided. He also longs for the Real Order, which refers, among other things, to the pre-natal period and the mother's body, but he has no access to it. Lacan holds that all the three orders are co-existent and inter-dependent. Significantly, Imaginary, Symbolic and Real, do not have their denotative meanings in Lacan. Each term refers to a specific mental stage of the subject, though the Lacanian stages are not strictly chronological as those of Freud's developmental stages.

Lacan's concept of desire is all inclusive; it encompasses

many of Freudian concepts like the libido, the Eros, the pleasure principle, and wish-fulfilment (Lacan 1968: 185). Depending upon the context, Lacan has emphasized one Freudian meaning or the other. On the whole, however, "for Lacan the fundamental driving force of the human subject, the dynamic power that propels him, is not libido or eros, as for Freud, but desire" (Muller and Richardson 1982:19). For this reformulation of Freud, Lacan has drawn on Hegel as interpreted by Alexandre Kojeve.

In *Phenomenology of Mind*, Hegel advances a theory of "desire for recognition" and illustrates it with the master-slave dialectic. Anthony Wilden's excerpt from the early Lacan's paraphrase of Hegel is helpful in this regard (Lacan 1968: 114):

> The very desire of man, [Hegel] tells us is constituted under the sign of mediation; it is desire to make its desire recognized. It has for its object a desire, that of the other, in the sense that there is no object for man's desire which is constituted without some sort of mediation—which appears in his most primitive needs; for example, even his food has to be prepared—and which is found again throughout the development of satisfaction from the moment of the master-slave conflict throughout the dialectic of labour ['Propos sur la causalitie psychique.' (1950:45)]

What is important in Hegel for Lacan is the principle of mediation. There is no direct and unmediated object for man's desire, because desire is always the desire of the other. In Lacanian terms, a subject as subject cannot desire; it is only as an other of his own subject that he desires. Further, the desire is for recognition of desire as desire. This complex quest for recognition can go to the extent of losing one's life. There should not be any real death because the quest itself will be lost if the subject chooses to die.

The Hegelian desire for recognition takes on a symbolic dimension in Lacan. For him the desire is mediated by language. As a matter of fact, the subject learns to experience his mother's absence as presence through language only. Freud explains this crucial moment with the game of *Fort* (gone) and *Da* (here) in *Beyond the Pleasure Principle*. With the advantage of hindsight, Lacan employs the structuralist notion of binarism, that is, of presence and absence and suggests that language becomes a complement to the child. Moreover, Lacan has advanced the idea of metonymic desire because the unconscious desire is trapped in the endless chain of signification without signifieds. There may be several substitutions for the object of desire but desire remains unquenchable and insatiable. Padmini's desire in *Hayavadana* is precisely such a metonymic desire and the transposition of the heads of Devadatta and Kapila is only a symptom of her desire.

A distinction is often made among need, demand, and desire. Need refers to the physical needs of the child such as milk and warmth for his existence. These needs can be satisfied by any person. The biological mother's presence is not obligatory. Demand, on the other hand, is directed against a particular object. It can also be fulfilled but it involves an inherent and inevitable ambiguity. Madan Sarup illustrates this ambiguity with the example of a mother giving a bar of chocolate to her child. (1989: 24) The child may feel happy about the chocolate but he cannot ascertain whether his mother's action can be attributed to love or hate for him. For the mother can satisfy the child to show her love as well as to stop him from crying. This inherent ambiguity in the mother's action compels the child to demand love and affection, which in turn becomes desire. A good example can be seen in Karnad's play *Tale-Danda* in Act One. When Kallappa, the king's bodyguard, receives a kick from the king and leaves, Bijjala, the king, says: "That sly bastard, I shall never know if he hasn't made an ass of me." (13) Kallappa recognizes the king's desire for being known as an invincible warrior but the king is not sure of such a recognition.

Identifying the insatiable desire as "the ultimate desire," Richard Harland says that "if the loss of individual selfhood is the ultimate fear, the confirmation of individual selfhood is the ultimate desire." (39) Unfortunately, there is no such self in reality. The sense of self felt by the subject is only an image as Lacan points out in the mirror stage. Harland further provides a systematic account of desire:

> Desire is caught in a multitude of mirrors: desire to take the place of the 'other' in desire (and love and admire 'I' from outside): desire to be what the 'other' desires (as when a woman desires to become the object a man desires); desire for the object's desire (as when a man desires a woman who is socially designated as desirable). Satisfiable need gets lost in the demand for love and admiration. (40)

Thus need changes to demand as demand changes to desire. Besides, the nature of desire is also altered by the entry of language into the child. Whether it is the desire to be the other, or the other's desire, or the object of the other's desire, the subject's desire for recognition dominates and consequently dooms him. Lacan's desire, then, is closely connected with the Freudian death-drive, which according to Lacan, originates from the Western culture with its glorification of individualism and capitalism, not only of making capitals (wealth) but also of unmaking capitals (heads).

If Jacques Derrida exposes the centreless structure and

if Michel Foucault discloses the centreless power structures, Jacques Lacan unmasks the centreless but structured subject. The Lacanian subject is in a perpetual state of lack attempting desperately to find unity, coherence, completion, perfection, and similar ideals both within and without. In a sense human desire springs from this lack. Mother, father, language, the Unconscious, and other agencies act as complements to the subject as he does to them. Of all the desires, however, the desire for recognition plays a vital role in the subject's search for completeness, which is the theme of Girish Karnad's *Hayavadana*.

Interestingly, Karnad the playwright himself has provided a Lacanian framework in *Hayavadana* in three significant words: "fate," "desire," and "lack." Whether Karnad has used them with a Lacanian awareness or by chance is anybody's guess. Their place of occurrence is also noteworthy. After blessing *Hayavadana* in his "search for completeness," the Bhagavata tellingly remarks in Act One: "Each one to his *fate*. Each one to his own *desire*. Each one to his own *lack*." (11; emphasis added) And then the Bhagavata narrates the main story without any further interruption. Later in Act Two, the Dolls too speak of Devadatta and Padmini similarly:

Doll I: Each one to his *fate*!
Doll II: Each one to her *problems*! (50; emphasis added)

These two passages reinforce the Lacanian framework of the eternal lack in human beings. Karnad's characters seek wholeness due to their divided self. Their fate, then is to meet with their own problems of identity, complicated relationships, and finally their own end.

It is important, however, to notice that the "lack" of

1985 text has been changed to "luck" in the 1995 text of *Hayavadana in Three Plays* (82). Whether "luck" is a right correction or a printer's devil, it may be suggested that luck and lack are curiously interchangeable. The "lack" of the human beings is their "luck" and their "luck" is their "lack." Similarly, "luck" and "fate" are closer in meaning. Since "lack" directly refers to the theme of the play, the 1985 text seems to be more authentic. Further, almost all the characters in *Hayavadana* are signifiers of the Lacanian lack and desire.

Strangely enough, Ganesha's image that is brought to the stage seems to be a symbol of the real Lacanian subject—incomplete, incoherent, fragmented, divided, and centreless. The only difference is that the human subject makes an incessant attempt to seek wholeness whereas the divine subject is not at all bothered about the incongruous appearance. Lord Ganesha is in the form of a man's body with an elephant's head, a broken tusk and a cracked belly. The God is not complete but mysteriously He is the "destroyer of incompleteness." (1) He is "the Lord and Master of Success and Perfection." (1) The Lord by His very physical appearance seems to indicate to his devotees that they should not search for completeness. If the mirrored image of the human subject is duplicitously whole and unified, the dramatized image of Ganesha projects the true Lacanian subject. It is a matter of critical speculation whether Lacan would have identified Ganesha and similar Hindu Gods as "letters" of his subject, for he has shown keen interest in the Upanishads.

The protagonist of the sub-plot, Hayavadana, has a human body and an equine head but he is not a god like Ganesha. Though he is born of a *gandharva* father, he is not one because he does not have divine powers like his father to change his own shape or that of others. He is not a man, nor a horse, though he has features of both. Hayavadana is, thus, incomplete but he is unable to accept his fate. Within the range of his experience, he desires to look like human beings in order that he may belong to their society. Hence, his search for completeness—a complete human being.

His lack/luck, unfortunately, is bad enough to change him into a complete horse, for the Goddess of Mount Chitrakoot does not wait to listen to his full prayer for becoming a full man. Through this change from bad to worse Karnad may ridicule the idea of the supremacy of head as Thomas Mann does in "The Transposed Heads": the law of head, face, identity, society, and so on is headless. For Lacan, however, the head or the body or both put together is incomplete and incoherent. Lord Ganesha seems to be aware of this Lacanian fact but Hayavadana, despite his horse sense, is unaware that incompleteness is the lot of the human beings. If Hayavadana is "an image of an average Indian citizen" as G.H. Nayak (1973: 105) suggests, he can also be an image of an average human being in general. Notably the question of completeness does not arise in Hayavadana after he loses his human voice. Blissfully, he lapses from the linguistic phase to the pre-linguistic phase.

Hayavadana's mother, the Princess of Karnataka, is not presented as a character in the play. Even then her marriage with the white stallion that carries the Prince of Araby is important from the viewpoint of Lacanian desire. Marital life is a physical, psychological, and social need. To fulfill this need, the Princess could have chosen one of the several suitors from different parts of the land who have assembled at the *svyamvara*. However, she insists on marrying the horse, who is mysteriously a *gandharva* cursed by god Kubera to become a horse. What is the source and exact nature of her desire?

The vulgar and reductive Freudian may hold that the Princess's is a case of zooeroticism and nymphomania. Can such a view explain the complexity of the problem? It is not exactly her biological need that bothers her. Further, it is not a satisfiable demand, though her father arranges for the socially unacceptable marriage. Therefore, it appears to be the desire born of the split between need and demand that compels the Princess to choose the horse instead of the horse rider in contrast to the Padmini of the main plot who often dreams and sings about a horse rider. When the horse becomes a Celestial Being after fifteen years of his life with the Princess, she demands him to become a horse again to go to heaven with him as he desires. When she is cursed to change into a horse, she has no more problem of desire as it happens in the case of Hayavadana.

Lacan (1968: 172) has suggested that animals, including chimpanzees, do not take pleasure in looking at their own image in the mirror. As a result, they do not have any desire for wholeness as human beings do. Both Hayavadana and his mother are disturbed by the desire for recognition so long as they have traces of human beings, especially language. Once they are turned into a complete horse, the Lacanian desire does not operate in them.

Then, it is possible to conjecture that both gods and animals do not suffer from the problem of misrecognition of their own image in the mirror. Consequently, they do not have to seek an imaginary wholeness which may bring them "harmony" and "happiness." But the ill-starred human beings, being what they are, are driven to search for the unattainable ideal In several cases, this impossible search ends in unavoidable destruction, which is performed by the protagonists of the main plot—Devadatta, Kapila, and Padmini.

It is Devadatta who is often caught in the tangle of desire, more than fifteen girls in two years as Kapila says. His desire for Padmini, however, seems to be destructive in its end. He is a pundit and a poet. Naturally, he is likely to have a latent desire for outshining Kalidasa and his *Shakuntalam*. His desire, then, is the desire for immortality in the Bloomian sense (Dhanavel 1993: 118-20). His latent desire surfaces strongly only when he sees Padmini. Thereafter, he develops the fatal desire for possessing her by marriage, allegedly for excelling Kalidasa. His desire is somehow fulfilled by Kapila, his bosom friend. When Devadatta is frustrated due to non-recognition of his desire by Padmini, he proceeds to execute his vow. He forgets his wife, his friend, and most importantly his desire for surpassing Kalidasa.

As the opportunity comes up in the forest, Devadatta goes to the Kali temple and commits suicide after uttering the following words:

> Bhavani, Bhairavi, Kali, Durga, Mahamaya, Mother of all Nature—I had forgotten my promise to you. Forgive me, Mother. You fulfilled the deepest craving of my life—you gave me Padmini—and I forgot my word. (28)

It is true that his desire is fulfilled temporarily but his "ego" is wounded permanently. As a result, he wounds/kills himself to get the recognition that he misses in life. Following the death of Kapila, both get their life by the grace of Kali. However, the problem of recognition, confirmation of selfhood, continues until all the three are dead.

The nature of Devadatta's desire for Padmini implies an ulterior motive other than her as an object of her desire. He wants her to be his muse, but she is not content to play this role. She has her own desire for recognition which is truly the ultimate desire for affirmation of her selfhood. Such a desire of Padmini is revealed clearly in her interaction with Kapila, who is on the negotiating mission for his friend's marriage. She is seen humming her favourite song "Here comes the rider—from which land does he come?" (16) Kapila's initial reaction is one of astonishment. Even before he recovers himself from his sense of beauty-shock, she starts grilling him. The wrestler who could catch his rival Nanda "in a crocodile-hold" is shattered by the sight of Padmini. She goes to the extent of checking even his eyesight.

Naturally, it is difficult for any man to "conquer" her. When Kapila is unable to make any headway in his mission, he surrenders to her in frustration:

Kapila [*looking around: aside*] No one here. Still I have to find her name. Devadatta must be in pain and . . . He will never forgive me if I go back now. [*Aloud*] Madam, please. I have some important work. I'll touch your feet . . .

Padmini [*eager*] You will? Really? Do you know, I've touched everyone's feet in this house some time or the other, but no one's ever touched mine? You will?

Kapila [*slapping his forehead as he sinks to the ground*] I'm finished—decimated—powdered to dust—powdered into tiny specks of flour. [*To Padmini*] My mother, can I at least talk to a servant?

Padmini: I knew it. I knew you wouldn't touch my feet. One can't even trust strangers any more. Allright, my dear son; I opened the door. So consider me the door-keeper. What do you want? (18-19)

Padmini never gives a chance to Kapila for overcoming her in this conversation. But then, Kapila is equally a real fighter. He will not give up his fight, even if he is decimated.

Then Kapila faces Padmini boldly and straight-forwardly. Only when he advances fearlessly and forcefully does she take to her heels calling after her mother. At this point itself, Kapila realizes that his delicate friend Devadatta is no match for her because only an iron man will suit her. The implication of Kapila's realization is not merely sexual: it includes Padmini's desire to be recognized as a person in her own right. She is a powerfully witty and wild woman as she proves herself to be throughout the play. She requires a man of similar temperament who will accept her as she is, not the serious and sulky scholar like Devadatta. Predictably, Devadatta and Padmini are not happy with each other in their married life. She makes a few efforts to accept her lot but the lingering presence of Kapila in their family changes the course of her life.

Padmini understands Kapila as much as he understands her but Devadatta understands neither of them nor himself. He is full of his books and discussions in which neither of them is so keen. Gradually, the cracks in the relationship of Padmini and Devadatta become stronger. In the forest where they take rest, they speak out their minds in asides. Padmini finds Kapila on the Fortuante Lady's tree "a Celestal being" and says "No woman could resist him." (26) So far Devadatta could not see his friend's "manly muscles" because he did not have Padmini's eyes. When he recognizes them, it is too late. He has no other choice but to commit suicide at the Kali temple. His problem is that he desires Padmini but she does not share in his desire for immortality. Perhaps, it is possible that her desire for recognition has already been recognized by Kapila in his first encounter itself. Further, it is also likely that the recognized desire of Padmini cannot be re-recognized again by Devadatta.

However, Kapila too commits suicide as a true friend of Devadatta. The fact is that the bondage between Devadatta and Kapila has been established prior to the introduction of

Padmini. A complementary relationship can be seen between them also: head + body = complete man. Padmini as a weak complement of Devadatta and as a strong complement of Kapila is a late arrival. Nevertheless, the crisis has to be faced. Padmini too would have died but for the interference of Goddess Kali who grants her wish to save the dead. In her confused state of mind, she bungles and waits for more suffering. The transposed Devadatta and Kapila, on the other hand, thank her because, as Kapila says, "Now we are blood-relations! Body relations!" and he considers the exchange of heads as a "gift." (35) While the desire of both Devadatta and Kapila has been to be one, to be unified, the desire of Padmini too is that they should be one head and heart. Apparently, she is happy with Devadatta's head and Kapila's body but time disenchants her. Devadatta and Kapila change gradually to their former shape as per the law of supreme head and accept their fate psychologically. But Padmini remains discontented due to her ultimate desire for affirmation of her selfhood. The recurrent song of the Female Chorus about "the thick yearning of the many-flowered lantana" (ibidem:11) symbolizes Padmini's mind.

That is why, Padmini does not hestitate to seek out Kapila, the man of her song and dream, in the forest. At first, Kapila is angry with her but accepts her. Later, he asks her: "Why have you come from him?" (56) She questions him in reply, "What do you want me to say?" The Bhagavata intervenes at this juncture and reveals the whole inner mind of Padmini:

> How could I make you understand? If Devadatta had changed overnight and had gone back to his original form, I would have forgotten you completely. But that is not how it happened. He changed day by day. Inch by inch. Hair by hair. Like the trickling sand. Like the water filling the pot. And

> as I saw him change—I couldn't get rid of you. That's what Padmini must tell Kapila. She should say more, without concealing anything, 'Kapila, if that *rishi* had given me to you, would I have gone back to Devadatta some day exactly like this? But she doesn't say anything. She remains quiet. (56)

The slow and gradual change in Devadatta has forced Padmini to see whether Kapila too would have changed in the same way. Padmini's is not, however, a scientist's curiosity to test his hypothesis but one of recognizing another human being's desire for recognition. When Kapila asks her again why she has come to him, she replies confidently, "I had to see you." (56)

It is possible to bank upon the speech of the Bhagavata for the view that Padmini desires Kapila physically as U.R. Anantha Murthy (1976: 40-41) does. Actually, Padmini's "desire is caught in a multitude of mirrors." It is the Lacanian desire for recognition that pushes Padmini to desire Kapila's desire because she finds her desire being desired by Kapila. Though she is married to Devadatta, Kapila too gradually moves towards her because his desire is being desired by her. In this way both of them complement each other and achieve a sense of wholeness, harmony, and happiness as is evident from the forest scene where Kapila fulfils more than of Padmini's desire by fetching a bunch of the Fortunate Lady's flowers about which she just expressed her interest. Therefore, she comes to the forest breaking the marital bond. Consequently, all the three die. While Devadatta and Kapila fight and kill themselves, Padmini immolates herself. Logically, the Lacanian desire leads to death which ends all desires.

The character of Kapila is intimately connected with both Devadatta and Padmini. If he is the complement of Devadatta as body, he is also the complement of Padmini as "person."

While Devadatta looks at him as a "slave," Padmini considers him as her "master." As Kapila plays both roles of master and slave, he seems to have much better understanding of himself and others. Once he is caught in the tangle of desire, he has no scope for escape from destruction. Padmini follows him into the deep forest, while Devadatta follows both. Kapila desires recognition of his desire from both and receives destruction from both. After all, desire in the sense of greed and passion is the root cause of evil as the Buddha would say. For Lacan, desire is not evil but the destiny of mankind.

If Hayavadana and the Princess of Karnataka regress to the pre-linguistic phase of animal life, and if Devadatta, Kapila, and Padmini return to the pre-natal phase of all life, that is death, the nameless child of Padmini progresses to the linguistic phase at the end of the play. He is not a normal child because he is usually withdrawn and morbid. However, when he hears the laughter and speech of Hayavadana, he too starts laughing and speaking. Thus he becomes "a full member of the family and of society " (Belsey 1980: 60) only after entering the Symbolic Order. Perhaps Hayavadana breaks the child's moribund attachment to his doll and facilitates him to come into the linguistic stage. The Child is incomplete without the human language whereas the horse is incomplete with the human language. Karnad effects a miraculous transfer of language from Hayavadana to the Child and projects them as complete beings, though he knows well that such a sense of completeness is merely wish-fulfilment. What Karnad seems to suggest is that the entry into and departure from language is a routine cycle for human beings. If the Unconscious is structured like a language, how else can the human beings that possess the Unconscious be structured?

While Lord Ganesha is presented on the stage as an image, an obligatory feature of the *Yakshagana* tradition, Goddess Kali is shown as a character in the play. The Mother of all Nature resides at Mount Chitrakoot. Once countless devotees used to visit her regularly but now she is neglected. The Bhagavata directs Hayavadana to her. Devadatta, Kapila, and Padmini come to her by chance en route to Ujjain. Surprisingly, the Mother is found sleeping and indifferent to the needs of her devotees. In fact, she brings about more suffering to them by her casual and non-committal blessings.

What seems to be important for her is her own desire for recognition. She feels unhappy with Devadatta because the latter had "promised his head to Rudra and his arms to me!" (33) Similarly, she is sore with Kapila for not recognizing her at all, for he "didn't even have the courtesy to refer to me." (33) Likewise, she is rather blunt in the treatment of Padmini. The Goddess alleges that Padmini is selfish and remains unconcerned about her problems after the transposition of heads. In case of Hayavadana, Kali is deliberately mischievous in making him a complete horse contrary to his wish to become a complete man. Evidently, the Mother of all Nature is not at all motherly and caring for her distressed children. Why does the Mother behave in these unexpected ways? The fact is that the Goddess is also in the human linguistic system which divides the "self" and institutes desire in the subject. Kali is divine but she is a human subject due to her human language.

Girish Karnad's *Hayavadana* is, then, a play of desire—a drama as well as a game of the desire for recognition. The Bhagavata and the Dolls provide the Lacanian framework of fate, desire, lack, and problems for both plots. Hayavadana searches for human completeness but attains animal completeness. His mother marries a horse and is cursed to become a horse. Both of them regress to the pre-linguistic stage of animal life where there is no problem of wholeness, nor recognition. Lord Ganesha, on the other hand, remains at the divine level. Though imcomplete and imperfect, He is paradoxically the destroyer of incompleteness as also the Master of Perfection. Significantly, He appears to be a true Lacanian subject without any illusion of wholeness. At the human level, Devadatta, Kapila, and Padmini are trapped in the *triangle* of desire for recognition. Padmini's metonymic desire is played out through the transposition of heads, leading to the tragic end of all the three. The Child of Padmini refuses to enter the linguistic stage. However, Hayavadana enables him to laugh and speak normally. His entry into language suggests the continuity of the endless chain of desire for recognition. Goddess Kali is unique in the sense that she is a divinity but suffers from the agony of desire for recognition because she speaks the human language. In all, the Lacanian desire for recognition is useful in understanding the complex motives of Karnad's characters in *Hayavadana* who move along the signifying chain of desire till they reach the nonverbal stage of speechlessness and death.

The Indian Imagination of Girish Karnad

Contemporary Indian drama can boast of a host of great playwrights like Badal Sircar, Mohan Rakesh, Vijay Tendulkar, and Girish Karnad. All of them are regional dramatists in the sense that they write their plays in the regional languages, Bengali, Hindi, Marathi, and Kannada, respectively. They have together produced in Karnad's words, "the best plays in the last thousand years" (Ramnarayan 15). Like the Irish playwright Samuel Beckett who wrote his immortal plays, *Waiting for Godot* and *Endgame,* in French and later translated them into English to become the unassailable icon of contemporary British drama, the Konkan Karnad has authored his monumental plays, *Tughlaq, Hayavadana, Naga-Mandala. Tale-Danda*, and *The Fire and The Rain* in Kannada and then rendered them into English to emerge as the emblem of a vibrant and rich contemporary Indian English drama for the whole world.

Karnad's incredible achievement has been possible due to his extraordinary dramatic genius and the wholesome opportunities he has had with gifted directors like B.V. Karanth, Alyque Padmasee, Ebrahim Alkazi, Satyadev Dubey, Om Shivpuri, and Shyamanand Jhalan. And most importantly, Karnad's creative imagination is thoroughly and originally Indian in every one of its blood cells, for he has declared courageously: "my three years in England had convinced me Western theatre had nothing to offer us" (Karnad

1989 b: 342). It would be appropriate and useful, then, to explore the characteristics of the Indian imagination, as delineated by V.K. Gokak and A.K. Ramanujan, in Girish Karnad's plays, especially *Hayavadana*, to arrive at a fairly objective assessment of this dramatic giant's achievement.

To define the phrase "Indian imagination" is to enter the labyrinth of the vast multicullural sub-continent of India and the dense thicket of Indian psychology, sociology, and anthropology. However, the pioneering efforts of V.K. Gokak and A.K. Ramanujan may be followed as signposts in this direction. In the illuminatig chapter on "Indian Literature as an Expression of Indian Culture" of his book *India and World Culture*, Gokak (1986: 106-19), used the phrase "Indian imagination" and suggested that it arises from the Indian setting encompassing the philosophical and religious beliefs, the flora and fauna, the historical developments, and the political, social, and scientific transformations.

Subsequently, Gokak (1978: 21-25) refined a wide variety of characteristics of the Indian imagination into a precise formulation in his paper on "The Concept of Indianness with Reference to Indian Writing in English." Raising two key questions, "Who is an Indian?" and "What is Indianness?," he combined the partial answers to them and observed concisely: "An Indian, then, is a person who owns up the entire Indian heritage and not merely a portion of it. This integral cultural awareness is an indispensable feature of Indianness." (24) Karnad was preparing himself assiduously to own up the British culture, but found himself "nailed to my past." (Karnad 1989b: 334) His playwriting, then, is the blood oozing out of the nailed and crucified Karnad. In fact, he is a living martyr in the cause of Indian drama.

If Gokak identified Indianness with the entire Indian culture, A.K. Ramanujan (41-58) located the concrete processes of the Indian way of thinking in his provocative and perceptive essay on "Is There an Indian Way of Thinking? An Informal Essay." According to him, there are three aspects of the Indian personality: (a) inconsistency, (b) inability to distinguish between the self and the other, and (c) particularism.

To elaborate further, inconsistency is not confined to certain contradictions within a person, as Ramanujan illustrates with his father's simultaneous belief in both the Gita and Bertrand Russell. It also includes hypocrisy by which he means that "Indians do not mean what they say, and say different things at different times." (44) Second, the Indian's inability to distinguish between the self and the other is due to the "underdeveloped" Indian ego which is rather magical and animistic, collectivistic and primitivistic. Finally, particularism is concerned with the Laws of Manu, which are highly context sensitive. It is well-known that there is no universal law for the Indians in Manu. For instance, justice for a *brahmin* is different from that of justice for a *kshatriya,* or a *vaisya*, or a *shudra.*

Ramanujan believes that these characteristics are the warp and woof of the Indian personality and society. Perhaps, Karnad is the first Indian dramatist to reflect the really typical Indian characteristics in his plays, as he has consciously resisted the influence of the Western theatre which fails to take cognizance of the Indian milieu in its entirety. That is why, the achievements of playwrights like T.P. Kailasam, Adya Rangacharya, Aurobindo Ghose, and Rabindranath Tagore are sadly limited. On various occasions (Karnad 1989a; Karnad 1995; Murthy 1995, among others) Karnad himself has drawn attention to this significant fact.

Indian imagination, then, is the holistic creative process

that is deeply rooted in the Indian soil in all shades and shapes: geographical, racial, linguistic, stylistic, thematic, cognitivistic, behaviouristic, and particularistic. For the discussion of these features in Karnad's plays, especially *Hayavadana*, however, a little more specific categories can be employed. These include subject matter, dramatic form, setting, myths and legends, literary allusions, habits and beliefs, karma and rebirth, caste, and language. What follows, then, is an analysis of the plays with reference to these nine aspects, among others, that constitute Karnad's Indian imagination.

A play in Two Acts, *Hayavadana* is Karnad's third play. He wrote it originally in Kannada in 1970 while he was on a Homi Bhabha Foundation Fellowship. The play was a grand success on the stage. Accolades came Karnad's way from many quarters, including the prestigious Kamaladevi Chattopadhyay Award for the best play of the year and the coveted Sangeet Natak Award for the best Indian playwright of the year. In response to the editor of the leading Indian theatre journal *Enact*, Rajinder Paul's suggestion, Karnad translated *Hayavadana* into English in 1971 and Paul published it in *Enact* in the same year. The English version was produced for the Madras Players in 1972 by Lakshmi Krishnamurthy and Yamuna Prabhu. In 1975 Oxford University Press published the play in the New Drama in India series with a benign introductory note from the renowned Kannada critic Kirtinath Kurtkoti. Since then, the play has been produced and performed in different translations and adaptations around the world with great success.

Karnad has invariably drawn the subject matter for his plays from the Indian culture: myths, legends, folk tales, and histories. If *Yayati* and *The Fire and the Rain* are based on two subsidiary stories from the *Mahabharata*, *Tughlaq*, *Tale-*

Danda and *Dreams of Tipu Sultan* (as yet unpublished) are concerned with three significant Indian historical personalities. If *Tughlaq* is known for his idealistic efforts to reform India politically and socially, and if Basavanna is remembered for his passionate endeavours to form a casteless society of *sharanas* in the twelfth century Karnataka, Tipu Sultan is cherished for his revolutionary zeal to challenge the British expansion. Both *Naga-Mandala* and *Hayavadana* are mythical and folkloristic. They are centred on women, children and the playwright. They are also rich and strong in their flavour of indigenous tradition. While *Naga-Mandala* is framed on two Kannada folk-tales, *Hayavadana* is moulded from the story of the *Vetalapanchavimsati*, of Thomas Mann, and of Karnad's invention.

Of all the plays of Karnad, *Hayavadana* is unique in its genesis. Of course, the main plot of Devadatta, Kapila, and Padmini is based on the *Vetalapanchavimsati*, a chain of puzzling stories in the larger chain of Somadeva's *Kathasaritsagara*. The original story has several versions, nearly six, two of which have incestual overtones that Karnad has carefully avoided (Raykar 341). Further, Karnad has made extensive use of Thomas Mann's enlarged version of the *Vetala* story in "The Transposed Heads," which is quite a long lyrical short story. Mann's story is not focussed on the riddle, nor on the wisdom of King Vikram but on the eternal philosophical question of mind-body dualism. Besides the motif of poetic influence, Karnad has added his own story of Hayavadana to the transposed heads and composed the play in the folk drama convention. Though Karnad has borrowed from both the Indian and German versions, his main aim has been to reflect on the psychological and sociological dimensions of the human desire for completeness, the unattainable complete happiness. Thus all the plays of Karnad have their roots in the Indian soil in terms of subject matter.

Even as he was growing up in Sirsi, a small town on the western ghats, Karnad was exposed to two distinct forms of drama: Company Natak theatre and *Yakshagana* theatre. When he went to Bombay for postgraduation, he came into intense and intimate contact with the Western theatre, especially the naturalistic theatre of Strindberg's *Miss Julie* as produced by Ebrahim Alkazi. Later when he stayed in England, Karnad had first hand knowledge of World Theatre. However, he has consistently banked upon the traditional Indian dramatic forms and conventions. Of course, there are certain combinations and permutations of all forms and techniques available to him but he is largely an Indian playwright with the strength of the Company Natak and *Yakshagana*.

Tughlaq, for instance, has been written in the episodic scenic divisions like Tennessee Williams's *A Streetcar Named Desire*. However, Karnad has used the Company Natak convention of the comic pairs, Aziz and Aazam. There is also the Company Natak technique of deep and shallow scenes, the interior of the palace and the exterior of the street. The cat and mouse game between Tughlaq and Aziz ends up in an ironical equation between the two inside the palace at the end of the play. Interestingly, there is an amalgamation of scenic and act divisions in *Tale-Danda* which explores the Company Natak form beyond the deep and shallow scenes. Perhaps, the subject matter of Basavanna demanded such radical exploration of the Brahmin's quarter, the inner chamber, the god's room as well as the courtesan's quarter. *Yayati*, *Hayavadana*, *Naga-Mandala*, and *The Fire and the Rain* experiment with the Sanskrit drama and the Yakshagana theatre. Clearly, the regional form has an edge over the other forms in Karnad's theatre.

By his own admission, Karnad (1989a: 99) is said to be

indebted to the epic theatre of Bertolt Brecht for the composition of *Hayavadana* in the *Yakshagana* tradition. Though the inspiration may have come from Brecht, the young Karnad's experience of Yakshagana plays during his boyhood at Sirsi cannot be ignored. The need for an essentially Indian experimental theatre during the 1960s is also a causative factor for Karnad to go back to *Yakshagana*. The immediate occasions, however, were Satyadev Dubey's desire for "a play in the Bhagavata style" (Paul 4) from Karnad, and B.V. Karanth's suggestion to make a play out of the story of the transposed heads instead of a film as Karnad was planning. It did not take long for the playwright to realize that the story could "make a marvellous theatre" (Karnad 1989a: 99). As the use of masks became a solution for transposing the heads, he began to employ all other conventions of *Yakshagana*: songs, music, the Bhagavata, Ganesha pooja at the opening, the Bhagavata vakyam at the end, stylized action, and others.

Strikingly, the *Yakshagana* techniques have beautifully blended with the themes of *Hayavadana*. For example, the worship of Lord Ganesha, the incomplete and imperfect god, a mere technical requirement of *Yakshagana*, becomes very significant thematically. Similarly, the Bhagavata, the traditional stage manager and narrator of *Yakshagana* plays multiple roles, including that of a listener to Hayavadana, who interrupts the main play. Of course, the Bhagavata performs his traditional functions of introducing the characters, filling the gaps by his narration, singing songs at appropriate situations, along with the Female Chorus, and helping the characters when necessary. He is also an important complement of the play, when he comments on the inner thoughts of the protagonists. His role of singing is shared by the Female Chorus, which is a notable innovation in Indian drama. Perhaps Karnad had in mind T.S. Eliot's *Murder in the Cathedral* where the Chorus consists of the women of Canterbury. While Eliot's Chorus sings its suffering and helplessness as Thomas Becket is going to be murdered, Karnad's Female Chorus ironically celebrates Padmini's desire and her voluntary death by fire. Karnad's Chorus is not the voice of traditional wisdom. Contrarily, it stands for the passionate feelings of Padmini and thus merges with the protagonist as an integral component of the character.

Another aspect of the convergence of technique and theme is the use of masks in case of Hayavadana and the two friends, Devadatta and Kapila. Mask is a technical device that can be used for certain characters and their characteristics. Hayavadana, for instance, has the mask of a horse head. The Bhagavata mistakes it for a mask and is annoyed with Hayavadana for disrupting the play with such foolery. When the Bhagavata is unable to pull out the mask, however, he realizes that the equine mask is Hayavadana's real head. This incident underscores Karnad's theme that "mask is face," that is, the mask one wears is no different from what one is. In *The Fire and the Rain* too, the mask of Vritra takes possession of Arvasu who is Vritra in his own life. The exchange of heads, that is, masks, between Devadatta and Kapila also proves that their individual real natures cannot be exchanged in reality.

Stylization of action is a major feature of *Yakshagana*. This technique constantly reminds the audience that they are watching a play and not a slice of life, resulting in some amount of distance between the play and the audience psychologically. Then, the audience will be able to think over the play for themselves critically. The theme of incompleteness, embodied by Lord Ganesha, Hayavadana, Padmini, Devadatta, and Kapila requires that the audience analyze their own incompleteness and accept it as a fact of life. The sword fight of Devadatta and Kapila, and the reaction of Padmini are stylized so as to increase the awareness of the audience about the problems faced by the characters in the play. As the action is slowed down in stylization, the characters are also frozen sometimes when the feelings of these characters are revealed by the Bhagavata. Thus, action, slow action, and stillness go to make the play of incompleteness in *Hayavadana*. In short, the *Yakshagana* conventions have enriched not only the thematic significance of the play but also Karnad's Indian dramatic imagination.

Except *Anjumallige* (1977), which is set in England, all the plays of Karnad have clearly recognizable Indian settings. To illustrate, *Tale-Danda* is set in the city of Kalyan, the capital city of King Bijjala's kingdom in Karnataka. The different parts of the city as well as the palace are distinctly identified: the Brahmin's quarter, the queen's chamber, the god's room, the inner chamber, the courtesan's quarter, and the front yard of the palace. In this respect, *Tale-Danda* is close to *Naga-Mandala* in which all actions take place in and around Appanna's house. *Tughlaq* and *Hayavadana*, by their very thematic nature, are bound to move to distant places from Delhi to Daulatabad, and from Dharmapura to the forest, respectively. Significantly, the places of origin are left behind in both these dramas.

The setting of *Hayavadana* is partly urban and partly rural: the city of Dharmapura and the forest of the Fortunate Lady tree. Within Dharmapura, Pavana Veethi, where Padmini has her house with the two-headed bird door frame, is prominently highlighted, when Kapila makes his negotiating trip there. While Devadatta's residence is taken for granted, Kapila's house is totally ignored. In the forest of the Fortunate Lady tree, the tree, the Kali temple, and later

Kapila's hut are adequately focussed. There is an unobtrusive thematic contrast between the urban and rural locales. In the city Padmini's passion is kept under control. When she goes to the forest on the Ujjain trip, her true feelings are expressed without reserve. Further, death is also courted in the forest only.

Of course, there are references to many other places like Ujjain, Karnataka, Banaras, Rameshwar, Tirupati, Gandhara, and Chitrapur. The holy places are mentioned by Hayavadana in the recounting of his story to the Bhagavata. Gandhara is invoked by both Kapila and Devadatta with reference to the wrestler from that place. Like Ujjain, Chitrapur also seems to be near Dharmapura. The forest, however, appears to be reserved for the tribal people only. At the end of the play, Actor I informs the Bhagavata that the tribal people did not accept Padmini's son and so the boy is brought back to the city. The urbanites do not come to the forest for shelter as it happens in *As You Like It*. Karnad's forest is truly a pastoral heaven but it does not have the benign influence of the Forest of Arden to change the heart of man for good. Contrarily, the human problems are complicated and end in bloodshed and death, though the ancient Indian sages attained their salvation in the wilderness. There is such an alternation between the city and the forest in *The Fire and the Rain* too. The violence of the wild is carried to the town for justice. Thus, the setting with the flora and fauna contribute its share to Karnad's Indian imagination, which is symbolized in the Fortunate Lady's tree.

Karnad believes in the Jungian collective racial consciousness (Chakravartee, 46) and so turns to the past habitually for both source materials and supporting materials. *Yayati*, *Tughlaq*, *Hayavadana*, *Naga-Mandala*, *Tale-Danda*, *The Fire and the Rain*, and other plays of Karnad are all literary excavations of the Indian collective past—the racial, the primitivistic, the mythical, the legendary, and the historical. Not surprisingly, Karnad's explorations of the past have a strong contemporary relevance. *Tughlaq* and *Tale-Danda*, for example, are acutely reflective of the contemporary political and social events, especially the Nehruvian era of disillusionment as well as the aftermath of the Mandal commission report and of the demolition of Babri Masjid over Rama Janma Bhoomi. As Karnad explains to Chakravartee, certain intricate problems are "perennial," because man does not learn from history. (49)

Subtle and constant juxtaposition of the past and present is a common feature of Karnad's dramatic art. To substantiate, the close friendship of Devadatta and Kapila in *Hayavadana* is said to be like that of Lava and Kusha, Rama and Lakshmana, and Krishna and Balarama. Lava and Kusha are Sita's sons born in the forest, when Rama throws her out of his palace due to his alleged suspicion of Sita's fidelity. Rama and Lakshmana are born of different mothers but the same father, that is, Dasaratha. Similarly, Krishna is born of Devaki but brought up by Yashoda. Rohini's son Balarama and Krishna grew up together. These are brotherly pairs of different kinds and famous for their strong fraternal friendship. In the same way, Devadatta and Kapila are supposed to be inseparable and mutually supporting friends.

It is natural, then, that Padmini is placed in the role of Sita when she is married to Devadatta. These three beings are portrayed like the ideal family of Rama, Sita and Lakshmana. Particularly, this ideal is more applicable to their forest life where Lakshmana is a protector of both Rama and Sita. Though Lakshmana has no other motive than providing security to Sita, she suspects him when he refuses to search for Rama who is after the false deer. Only then, he draws the line of protection called Lakshman-rekha and leaves Sita alone against his wish. Thereafter, it becomes easier for Ravana to appear as a mendicant before Sita and carry her off.

What happens in *Hayavadana* against this epic background is amusingly ironical. First, Padmini is not won by Devadatta but by Kapila. Then it is Padmini who takes away Kapila to the Rudra temple in front of Devadatta. Again, it is Padmini who decides to join Kapila in the forest, when she is disenchanted with the weak Devadatta. As for Devadatta, he does not really trust his friend. Besides, he brings a sword to fight with him and to kill themselves, forgetting about the woman. Though Kapila is attracted to Padmini, he seems to have some self-control. He tells himself in an aside "get a tight hold on yourself. You are slipping, boy, control yourself Don't lose that hold." (23) He is not only strong and talented but also fairly honest. He is naive enough to suggest that they could live together like the Pandavas and Draupadi of the *Mahabharata*. However, Padmini chooses to be silent and then fall into the fire in the tradition of *sati*. Whether or not the tragic end is inevitable remains an open question. The playwright resolves the problem dramatically, but leaves it to the audience to ponder over.

There are a few more mythical references which call for elucidation. Though the story of Hayavadana was invented by Karnad, it is imbued with a strong mythical base. Hayavadana's father is a *gandharva* in the form of a horse due to the curse of Kubera, the god of wealth. Lord Kubera's wife, Yakshini, is mentioned by Kapila in the list of heavenly beauties that he compares Padmini with. The significance of Lord Kubera lies in the divine anger against a *gandharva*, which results in the birth of Hayavadana with a horse head. Indra, the god of Heaven, is referred to in the Bhagavata's song after Devadatta and Kapila decide about their sword fight. The "crack on the earth's face" is "exactly like Indra's smile" (61), sings the Bhagavata. The god's smile, then, is sinister and ill-boding, for Indra is notorious for coveting other men's wives. Vishakha in *The Fire and the Rain* mockingly speaks about the "thousand eyes" of Indra, which are supposed to have come to him due to the curse of sage Agasthya, whose wife Ahalya Indra seduced. The implications are obvious. King Vikram is the legendary figure that is bound to appear in *Hayavadana* to give his wise verdict on the fate of the protagonists, if not directly. Clearly Vikram's wisdom is not applicable to the modern society. If so, what wisdom is available to Karnad to solve the problem of complete perfection and happiness faced by his characters?

Of all the mythical and legendary figures, goddess Kali of Mount Chitrakoot plays a decisive role in both the plots of *Hayavadana,* for she appears as a character in the play, though briefly. First, she is indifferent to the suicides of Devadatta and Kapila but interferes in Padmini's attempt to kill herself. Then she helps Padmini to revive the dead men but is indifferent when the heads are mixed up. The Goddess plays a negative role in the case of Hayavadana too. She prevents him from committing suicide but does not allow him to complete his prayer for a complete man. Contrarily, she transforms him into a horse but does not remove his human voice. Thus, both Padmini and Hayavadana are tortured by the Goddess for no specific reason but her lethargy and perpetual stupor. Obviously, Karnad has painted Kali black to portray the sufferings of human beings in an indifferent and hostile world. The playwright's ironical juxtaposition of the past and present resembles the modernist technique of James Joyce and T.S. Eliot. While Eliot became an exponent of his faith in Anglicanism, Karnad continues to question Hinduism:

The references to Lava and Kusha, Rama and Lakshmana, Krishna and Balarama, Rama-Sita-Lakshmana as well as the Pandavas and Draupadi are surely literary as they are part of the great Indian epics. They are, however, rooted in the Indian myths. And so the literary allusions here are restricted to authors like Kalidasa and Bhasa that Karnad has cited in *Hayavadana Tughlaq* too has certain references but they are mostly Persian and Greek. Nevertheless, Karnad's Indian imagination is no less remarkable because these non-Indian references are appropriate for the scholar that Tughlaq was. Perhaps the political allegory of Nehru who was well-versed in world literature suggested them. In comparison, *Naga-Mandala*, *Tale-Danda*, and *The Fire and the Rain* have least literary references.

Karnad's allusion to Kalidasa and his *Shakuntalam* is very strong, if not pervasive, in *Hayavadana*. Being a poet, Devadatta wants to outshine Kalidasa but he needs a muse, that is, Padmini. Hence he swears that he will offer his head to Lord Rudra and his arms to Goddess Kali, if he is able to marry Padmini. That the marriage impelled by a literary ideal turns disastrous is a different matter altogether. The second reference is to Vatsyayana and his *Kamasutra* where he has described a class of women called Padmini. Vatsyayana is as important as Kalidasa for the play because Karnad too has depicted a class of Indian women who are seeking fulfilment outside marriage.

The earliest known Sanskrit playwright Bhasa is mentioned by Devadatta in the context of a misunderstanding between him and his wife. A great scholar that he is, he likes to read aloud one of Bhasa's plays to Padmini alone but Kapila joins in. Significantly, the play in question is not identified by Karnad, though Bhasa is credited with as many as thirteen plays of which the most famous is *Svapnavasavadatta* (The Dream of Vasavadatta). Bhasa is said to have been "a keen observer of human nature, humorous, witty and great optimist" (Saletone 213). Contrarily, Devadatta is unlike the playwright that he enjoys reading to his wife. He does not have any "sense of humour" (24), as Padmini points out in the same context. He is not an "optimist," nor "a keen observer of human nature." Devadatta seems to be just an empty, verbose, and vain brahmin.

Perhaps the assessment of Devadatta by U.R. Anantha Murthy (1976: 37-43) is valid to some extent, if he is merely a figure of mockery rather than a real representative of head. Devadatta's knowledge of Kalidasa is evident but of Bhasa, it is negligible. If the autobiographical connection of Karnad with Devadatta (Dhanavel 1993: 118-20) is explored further, it can be observed that Bhasa's plays were mostly adaptations of episodes from the *Mahabharata* and the *Ramayana* just as Karnad has done in *Yayati, Hayavadana*, and *The Fire and the Rain*. In this sense, Karnad may well be called the Bhasa of modern Indian drama.

A number of the Indian habits and beliefs are reflected in Karnad's plays. In *Naga-Mandala*, Appanna marries Rani but locks her up in his house and carries on his affair with his concubine. He is notoriously promiscuous but expects his wife to be chaste. He goes to the extent of lodging a complaint with the elders of the village for justice. Such a hypocritical attitude is common in many parts of the country, though women are liberated to a great extent now. Aziz the scoundrel in *Tughlaq* is appointed a state officer for tampering with the law and cozening the crown. Such scandalous persons are very much active in the contemporary political scenario. The brahminical tendency to keep the king under priestly control at any cost, even if it means brutal usurpation of power, is sharply focussed in *Tale-Danda*. Sovideva, the son of Bijjala and Rambhavati, is crowned forcibly, after being pulled out of the courtesan's quarter, and Bijjala is dethroned cunningly by the crooked priest Damodara Bhatta.

In these subtle exposures of the undesirable habits, Karnad excels as a satirical and humorous playwright, though his attack is never as savage as Ben Jonson's, nor as bitter as Bernard Shaw's. Further, there are very light-hearted and genially ironical situations which simply exhibit the contradictions, giving scope for immense laughter. The horse-headed Hayavadana points to the lack of civic sense in Actor I who sits on the roadside to relieve himself. Likewise, the Bhagavata reveals the drunken life of the lower classes through Actor I who swears that he has not been near a toddy shop. The Hindu custom of taking vows to please gods and goddesses with suitable offerings is also brought to light. Particularly, the hair-offering to Lord Balaji at Tirupati is ridiculed ironically as Hayavadana loves his mane and so skips the God of riches. There are many other instances in *Hayavadana* but these are representative of Karnad's perception of Indian reality.

A.K. Ramanujan's observation on the Indian characteristic of inconsistency and hypocrisy is largely true. Devadatta does not like the Ujjain trip, but he never tells his wife, nor his friend, in black and white. Instead, he goes on sulking and pretending to care for the health of his wife. At one point, Padmini explodes when the situation is unbearable:

> What's happened to you today? At other times you are so full of your books, you even forget to wash your hands after a meal. But today you've been going on and on all morning. (20)

Even after this direct angry remark, Devadatta carries on with his hypocritical attitude. When she is disgusted with him, Padmini volunteers to put off the trip. However, she cannot bear the sight of Kapila sinking as he learns about the called off trip. Like Devadatta, Kapila too indulges in such pretentious actions. He dies not so much for the sake of friendship as for fear of punishment. Surprisingly, it is the Goddess who openly criticizes all the three of them for their unhealthy habits.

Comparatively, Padmini is brave and forthright but she too is not free from hypocrisy. She is well aware that she wants a man of sound brain and sound body. She is also conscious that she cannot have such a single person, though she has her wish fulfilled for a short period while Devadatta has Kapila's body. Later when she is disillusioned, she persuades Devadatta to go to Ujjain fair on the pretext of buying new dolls for their son. She refers to the belief that it is unlucky to keep torn dolls at home. But her real motive is to be left alone so that she can venture to the forest and meet Kapila. She requests the Bhagavata to keep her son as the son of Kapila in the forest and then send him to the city as Devadatta'a son. She may have her own reasons but she is no different from Devadatta and Kapila in her inconsistency and hypocrisy.

Of all the beliefs, karma, the timeless chain of cause and effect relationships, stands out as the foremost Indian characteristic. It is the fate of Yayati to be cursed to old age when his life with Sharmishtha is solemnized. It is the fate of Kurudavva, in *Naga-Mandala*, to be born blind. It is the fate of the *sharana* movement of Basavanna, in *Tale-Danda*, to be dissolved. Though *Tughlaq* deals with a Muslim king, the Hindu fate hangs in the air. It is the karma of India to have had Tughlaq as a king, as it is his own karma to have been ruined by his own lofty idealism. The dream rose garden, which he has had built up so assiduously, is now filled up with heaps and heaps of counterfeit copper coins. Worst of all, he is compelled by circumstances to accept a common rogue as the holiest man. It is the karma, the irony of fate, that adds a special flavour to Karnad's plays.

The invincible karma of *Hayavadana* is suggested in the very appearance of Lord Ganesha and in the Bhagavata's song of praise and prayer. It gets focussed in the dialogue between the Bhagavata and Hayavadana. In fact, the Bhagavata represents the ancient karmic wisdom in all his sayings and doings. He tries to explain away that Hayavadana might have done some wrong in the past, indicating rebirth, to be born with an equine head in this life. On the other hand, Hayavadana represents the extreme of modern rational knowledge. The conflict between the ancient and the modern, karma and individual freedom, Sanskrit and Kannada or any other regional language for that matter, old and young, religion and science, high caste and low caste, and many other dichotomies is evident throughout the play. Karnad's own preference in these categories can easily be identified by a tonal study of *Hayavadana* and other plays. *Tale-Danda*, for instance, is a portrayal of the struggle against brahminism, though Basavanna, the founder of the *sharana* movement is a brahmin himself. A similar theme is also explored further in *The Fire and the Rain*. Undeniably, the influence of U.R. Anantha Murthy's great novel *Samskara* is noticeable in Karnad.

This conflict, interestingly, provides plenty of opportunities for Karnad to reveal his humorous genius. When the Bhagavata asks Hayavadana why he did not prevent the torture on him as the Bhagavata and Actor I try to pull out his horse head, Hayavadana earnestly replies:

> All my life I've been trying to get rid of this head. I thought—you with all your goodness and *punya* . . . if at least you managed to pull it off . . . (7)

While the Bhagavata habitually slips into the karma theory, Hayavadana stubbornly refutes it over and again. After his experiments and encounters with all kinds of holy places and holy men, Hayavadana has come to understand that man is responsible for his own actions, an existentialist position with which Karnad is well-acquainted. However, the play-wright's position seems to be closer to Herman Hesse's novel *Siddhartha*, a variety of atheist Buddhism. The understanding is that each individual has to work out his own salvation, if there is any, diligently. It is a view shared by the great intellectuals like T.S. Eliot. Surprisingly, there is hardly any reference to the Buddha as a viable solution in Karnad's plays, as it is evident in Eliot's *The Waste Land* and *The Cocktail Party*. The ending of *The Fire and the Rain*, how-ever, seems to echo *The Waste Land* with reference to the interpretation of *Da*, which is similar to the interpretation of the arrival of rains in Karnad's play.

The word fate is often used in the play by the major characters, including the Bhagavata. While the Bhagavata ac-cepts it as a given, Hayavadana continues to question the premise of fate until he loses his power of speech at the end of the play, perhaps, suggesting that those who ask ques-tions untiringly are silenced in some way or the other. Devadatta and Kapila too accept their fate, though Kapila resists at one point, before the great rishi's verdict on the husband question is reported by the Bhagavata. In course of time, however, he regrets his rash action. He even corrects Padmini's claim that her son is his son too, saying "I'm Kapila, Padmini. I didn't accept it that day. But I accept it now. I'm Kapila." (54)

Padmini's unquenchable desire for completeness is too powerful to allow her to accept her fate. She is courageous enough to question Goddess Kali as to why she did not prevent the men from their suicide. She is strong enough to reach out to the forest where Kapila resides. She is equanimous enough to enter the sacrificial fire. Her unmitigated regret is she has no option to wish for the same husband in her next birth. Nevertheless, the Bhagavata describes her as *pativrata*, a self-sacrificing woman dedicated to the service of her husband. Who is she? Who is her husband? What is her fate? are questions that remain unanswered. Probably Karnad feels that such questions are better to be swept under the carpet, as the Story says in *Naga-Mandala*, though the playwright himself cannot remain contented with unsolved questions.

Karma and rebirth are closely inter-related terms, though they do not mean the same. There are frequent references to the past, present, and future as a cycle of birth and rebirth. The present identity crisis of Hayavadana is attributed to some mistake in his past life by the Bhagavata. His Gandharva father's equine life of fifteen years is due to the curse of Lord Kubera for some misdemeanour. Devadatta praises his friend Kapila as a rarity: "One has to collect merit in seven lives to get a friend like him." Thus merits and demerits are cumulatively accrued in the cyclical process of birth, death, and rebirth. Kapila's error in this life is to covet his friend's wife and so he loses his friend. He begs Devadatta to accept him at least in the coming life. This belief system of karma and rebirth provides an essential fibre for the Indian imagination of Karnad.

The major factor in the dispensation of Manu, the Hindu law-giver is caste. It is considered to be the central characteristic of particularism in A.K. Ramanujan's concept of Indian way of thinking. It is also significant for Karnad (1989a:92) who has studied the "geography of an Indian society" for producing genuinely great Indian plays.

Karnad has seriously sought to capture the stratified society even in *Tughlaq*. Aziz the dhobi and Aazam the petty thief belong to the lower classes, for occupation and caste cannot easily be separated in India. Interestingly, Aziz masquerades as a brahmin called Vishnu Prasad to get justice from the King who has confiscated the brahmin's property. That the Muslims also had fallen into the *varnashrama* seems to be suggested in this episode, for the King is held guilty and justice meted out to the "brahmin." Whether a *shudra* would have got such dealing from the King is doubtful. What is striking about Aziz is that he has the extraordinary courage to tell the Sultan on his face: "What if I am a dhobi, your majesty? When it comes to washing away filth, no saint is match for a dhobi." (82) Though Aziz is a Muslim, he seems to be close to Kapila in Hayavadana, for both display greater intellect and powers than what is expected of them.

Even a deceptively simple play like *Naga-Mandala* does not fail to portray the *varna* idiom of the Indian society. A close reading of the play suggests that the man, that is the playwright, the Flames, the Story, Kurudavva, and Kappanna are drawn from the shudra communities. While Kurudavva tells her son about the place where he keeps his plough, a tool of the shudra, Appanna says to himself that he will bring an "untouchable" to bury the dog that is bitten to death by Naga. Appanna does not appear to be a brahmin, nor a vaisya, nor a shudra, though Kurudavva claims that she was the best friend of Appanna's mother. Perhaps he is a kshatriya who can afford to keep a wife at home and a concubine elsewhere without doing anything for his livelihood, a Jamesian character par excellence.

The perennial problem of caste is the central theme of *Tale-Danda*. Basavanna founds a casteless society of *sharanas*, devotees of Lord Shiva, but founders finally when a shudra boy is married to a brahmin girl. The King's caste is also prominently highlighted. Bijjala is not a real kshatriya for his ancestors were barbers. To be considered kings, his ancestors had "bribed generations of Brahmins with millions of cows." Bijjala adds: "All this so they could have the caste of kshatriyas, branded on their foreheads . . . one's caste is like the skin on one's body. You can peel it off top to toe, but when the new skin forms, there you are again: a barber—a shepherd—a scavenger!" (33) Modern Indian history also records a similar case of purchase of caste by the Maratha kings. In the post-independent India caste continues to play a crucial role in education and employment as well as government making and unmaking.

In *Hayavadana* the Indian varna system is polarized between head and body. Devadatta, the scholar-poet, represents the head and Kapila, the ironsmith, symbolizes the body. Despite the social distance between them, they are presented as bosom friends. Ironically, it is the shudra who manages to get Padmini, the vaishya girl, for the brahmin as his wife. The whole situation becomes complicated when Padmini and Kapila begin to appreciate each other's feelings. With all his poetry, logic and scholarship, Devadatta is not as charming as the illiterate and rough Kapila. When the transposed Devadatta reverts to his original brahmin shape, Padmini is disillusioned and leaves for the forest to be happy with Kapila. But Devadatta follows them soon to bring about the destruction for all the three. They cannot live like the Pandavas and Draupadi in the *Mahabharata* because they do not have the divine sanction of Lord Krishna.

A Norwegian playwright like Henrik Ibsen can write *A Doll's House* with the heroine walking out of her husband's house. An Indian playwright like Karnad cannot end his *Hayavadana* with the separation of Padmini from Devadatta and union with Kapila for various reasons, especially caste consideration. Perhaps, Karnad has attempted to play with the ending of *Naga-Mandala* in its second version. The Naga is revived and kept alive in Rani's tresses. The hunter girl is killed by her own husband and brother in *The Fire and the Rain* because she decides to live with an outcaste brahmin. Karnad's women are full of desires and dreams but they cannot live happily because they are denied their right to live with the man of their choice. In all cases, caste and male dominance prevail but the perspective of the oppressed and downtrodden is firmly inscribed by Karnad.

The account of Karnad's Indian imagination is incomplete without its linguistic manifestation in words, phrases, and idioms along the social and occupational lines. For language in general is indicative of the speaker's regional, social, and occupational origin. In India, caste also plays a crucial role in the language of a person irrespective of his social standing. In addition, there is the phenomenon of Indian English too.

Since Karnad does not write his plays in Indian English, it cannot be expected of him to mirror the same in his plays. Hence, Karnad has used "Standard English" for his translations in its spoken form. Surprisingly and strangely, however, the reader does not feel that he is encountering the English language in Karnad's plays. The subject matter, dramatic form, setting, myths and legends, literary allusions, habits and beliefs, and the social set-up are all so Indian that the reader feels at home with the plays, including *Tughlaq*. Obviously, the implied reader (theatre-goer) is an educated person with a literary background.

All the plays save *The Fire and the Rain* have Indian words in their title: Yayati, Hayavadana, Naga-Mandala, and Tale-Danda. There was no reason why Karnad should translate *Agni Mattu Male* into English as *The Fire and the Rain*. But he has done it, though he is aware of the severe loss of the most important dichotomies dominant in all his plays—the oppositions between the brahmin and the shudra which take on a host of other connotations (see Karnad 1998: 63). This oppositional theme is not explicit in the titles of other plays, though they deal with it. Karnad is against the totalitarian and hegemonic view of India as a monolithic entity but he has surrendered the Kannada identity of Mattu and Male in *The Fire and the Rain*. Whether he was afraid of losing popularity with *Tale-Danda* is known to him only. Though he has not embraced Sanskrit, he has depended on English, which also has the potential to act as a monolith. Probably this is the typical problem of the lower caste South Indian.

However, the Sanskrit origin of the titular words except *Tughlaq* gives the unmistakable Indian flavour to Karnad's plays. Further, he has used Indian words freely within the plays. Even *Naga-Mandala*, based on two simple Kannada folk tales, for instance, has words like kusbi and yaksha. Besides caste names like holeyas, madigas, and dohas, the word *sharana* is frequently employed in *Tale-Danda* almost like a counterpoint to the music of caste politics. Understandably, *Tughlaq* contains more of Persian and Arabic words but they do not in any way diminish Karnad's Indian imagination. Conversely, they throw light on the multicultural dimension of India.

Dealing with a Sanskrit scholar, *Hayavadana* has occasions for liberal use of Sanskrit words. Further, there are chunks of quotations, especially when Devadatta and Kapila sing of the beauty of Padmini. Even the ordinary people like the Bhagavata, the Female Chorus, and Hayavadana use such common words as *rishi, punyasthana, pativrata, puja, puranas, gandharva, mangalaratri, alpanas, arati, makarandas, jacarandas*, and *sati*. When Hayavadana sings the National Anthem by both Rabindranath Tagore and Bankim Chandra Chatterjee, the audience is not only amused but also instructed.

In addition to the words of Indian origin from Sanskrit, Bengali, and Hindi, it is noticed that Karnad has reflected the use of inclusive pronouns like "our" which in the Indian linguistic use may mean "your" or "my." Such a characteristic is found more in Kapila than in Devadatta. In an aside Kapila says, "It does look as though this sixteenth girl has really caught our Devadatta in her knot." (14) In another instance, Karnad uses the royal "we" in his response to Devadatta, "No, no—we might upset sister-in-law more then with our noise." (23) The implication seems to be that Padmini is also sister-in-law for Devadatta, which she is after all when she considers her son as Kapila's son. This extensive use of pronoun is an aspect of the Indian's inability to distinguish between the self and the other that A.K. Ramanujan has identified as the second characteristic of the Indian way of thinking.

Further, there are some prominent Indian idiomatic and proverbial expressions which Karnad has faithfully translated into English. Flame 1 tells Flame 3 in the Prologue of *Naga-Mandala* that "He [her master] is convinced his wife has a hole in her palm, so he buys all the groceries himself." (2) The Indian belief is that a person who spends money carelessly is said to have a hole in his palm between the fingers. Similarly, Haralaya tells Basavanna about his son

Sheelavanta, who is instructed by his mother Kalyani to touch the feet of the elders: "He's grown into a proper buffalo. Still needs to be told everything." (36) A grown up but ignorant boy is said to be a buffalo.

Several such Indian expressions are seen in *Hayavadana*. When Padmini tries to clear Devadatta's suspicion about her fidelity, she tells him, "You have no sense of humour." He replies, "It's humour for you. But it burns my insides." (21) "Burning insides" refers to the angry and frustrated mood of a person. Likewise, finding Kapila motionless, though she repeatedly urges him to get ready for the Ujjain trip, she bursts out, "Why are you standing like a statue?" (24) Another example is the expression that the Bhagavata uses on seeing Hayavadana at the end of the play: "Well well, you'll live to be a hundred." (65) These expressions may not be strictly idiomatic and proverbial according to the English conventions but they are commonly employed traditional utterances in the Indian languages, especially the South Indian languages of Tamil, Telugu, Kannada, and Malayalam. In fact, when a non-Kannada South Indian reads Karnad's English versions, he may feel that he is reading plays in his own language. Though the language is English in every way, the ethos of Karnad's plays is entirely Indian. What greater achievement can be expected of Girish Karnad?

Karnad's unique status as the greatest Indian English playwright, then, lies in his exemplary Indian imagination. A Konkan writing his plays in Kannada, translating them into English, and becoming a national and international playwright of eminent stature is an extraordinary Beckettian phenomenon. While Samuel Beckett remained an author, Karnad held the Chairmanship of Sangeet Natak Akademi. Of course, Beckett was awarded the Nobel Prize for Literature in 1969. It is unlikely that such a recognition for Karnad is far away.

because his genuine and typical Indian imagination is at bottom truly and profoundly universal.

The characteristics of Indian imagination as derived from both V.K. Gokak and A.K. Ramanujan are broadly subject matter, dramatic form, setting, myths and legends, literary allusions, karma and rebirth, caste, and language. All these nine features have been illustrated with reference to *Tughlaq*, *Hayavadana*, *Naga-Mandala*, *Tale-Danda*, and *The Fire and the Rain*. Other plays like *Yayati*, *Anjumallige*, *Hittina Hunja* and the latest *Dreams of Tipu Sultan* have been referred to wherever possible, as they are not yet available for the public in Karnad's own translations. Of all these plays, however, *Hayavadana* is considered to be the most representative play of Karnad's Indian imagination. One or the other aspect is missing or almost negligible in other plays, but *Hayavadana* manifests all of them and appropriately occupies a pre-eminent position in the Karnadian canon as well as in the Indian drama of all times. In fact, it is a condensed reverse epic of the great Indian epics, the *Mahabharata* and the *Ramayana*. For it does not leave out any domain of Indian or even universal experience—religion, politics, family, education, career, friendship, motherhood, poetry, drama, urban and rural life, man's eternal quest, and many more—from its dramatic micro-scope. The play includes the very birth, growth, and death of imagination, especially for the development of Indian drama. In this sense, *Hayavadana* is to Indian drama what James Joyce's *Ulysses* is to the Western novel. As *Ulysses* is the first best novel of the twentieth century, according to the Random House Committee, so is *Hayavadana* the first best drama of this century for India.

Karnad the playwright has excavated the Indian imagination from Bhasa through Kalidasa to Badal Sircar and Vijay Tendulkar and elevated it to the firmament of World

Drama with vital infusion from the double plot of William Shakespeare, the comic genius of Moliere, the social problems of Henrik Ibsen, the dramatic lyricism of Anton Chekhov, the naturalism of John Strindberg, the symbolic expressionism of Eugene O'Neill, the epic theatre of Bertolt Brecht, the religious quest of T.S. Eliot, the mythical and historical reinterpretations of Jean Anouilh and many more. Karnad's eclectic and synthetic approach to Indian drama has enabled him to portray the contemporary psycho-religious, socio-political, and literary-cultural turmoils authentically and admirably. Man does not learn from history but some individual men and women do. Of these fortunate few in India, Girish Karnad is the fountain of the vibrant Indian imagination from where has sprung his monumental plays of which, undoubtedly, the foremost is *Hayavadana*.

Works Cited

Abrams, M.H. 1993. *A Glossary of Literary Terms*. 6th ed. Bangalore: Prism Books.

Bandiste, D.D. 1996. *New Humanism: A Revolutionary Philosophy*. New Delhi: New Age International.

Belsey, Catherine. 1980. *Critical Practice*. London: Methuen.

Bhatta, S. Krishna. 1987. *Indian English Drama: A Critical Study*. New Delhi: Sterling.

Bloom, Harold. 1990-1991. "The Art of Criticism I" [An interview with Bloom by Antonio Weiss]. *Paris Review* 118:179-232.

______. 1987. "[An Interview with] Harold Bloom." In *Criticism and Society*, ed. Imre Salusinzky, 45-73. London: Methuen.

______. 1979. *The Flight of Lucifer: A Gnostic Fantasy*. New York: Farrar, Straus & Giroux.

______. 1975. *A Map of Misreading*. New York: Oxford University Press.

______. 1974. "Coleridge: The Anxiety of Influence. " In *Literary Criticism: Idea and Act*, ed. Willam K. Wimsatt, 506-20. Berkeley: University of California Press.

Chakravartee, Moutushi. 1991. "Moutushi Chakravartee talks to Girish Karnad." *Tenor* 7 (September): 46-50.

Dhanavel, P. 1999. "The Humanistic Vision of Girish Karnad." In *Contemporary Indian Literature in English: A Humanistic Perspective*, ed. Mithilesh K. Pandey, 76-87. New Delhi: Kalyani.

______. 1997. "Girish Karnad's *Hayavadana*: A Study in Condensation." *The Quest* 11: 2 (December): 13-19.

______. 1993. "The Romance of Influence: A Bloomian Perspective on Girish Karnad's *Hayavadana*." *Indian Journal of American Studies* 23: 1 (Winter): 118-20.

Dhawan, R.K. 1999. "Girish Karnad: The Man and the Writer." In Dodiya: 11-20.

Dodiya, Jaydip Singh, ed. 1999. *The Plays of Girish Karnad: Critical Perspectives*. New Delhi: Prestige.

Freud, Sigmund. 1960. *Introductory Lectures on Psychoanalysis*, trans. and ed. James Strachey. New York: Liveright.

Gokak, V.K. 1986 [1972]. "Indian Literature as an Expression of Indian Culture." In *India and World Culture*, 106-19. New Delhi: Sahitya Akademi.

_____.1978. "The Concept of Indianness with Reference to Indian Writing in English." In *Indian Writing in English*, ed. Ramesh Mohan, 21-

25. Madras: Orient Longman.

Gopalie, S. 1971. "Playwright in Perspective." *Enact* 54 (June): 6-8.

Gowda, H.H. Anniah. 1973. "Karnad's *Tughlaq* and Ramanujan's *Relations.*" *Literary Half-Yearly* 14: 1 (January): 3-10.

Harland, Richard. 1987. *Superstructuralism: The Philosophy of Structuralism and Post-structuralism*. London: Methuen.

Kalidasa. 1960. *Sakoontala*, trans. Sir Monier Monier-Williams. In *World Drama*, Vol. I, ed. Barrett H. Clark, 169-226. New York: Dover.

Karnad, Girish. 1998. *The Fire and the Rain*. Translated by the author. New Delhi: O.U.P.

_____. 1995 [1994]. *Three Plays: Naga-Mandala, Hayavadana, Tughlaq*. New Delhi: O.U.P.

_____. 1993. *Tale-Danda*. Translated by the author. New Delhi: Ravi Dayal Publisher.

_____. 1990. *Naga-Mandala: Play with a Cobra*. Translated by the author. New Delhi: O.U.P.

_____. 1989a. "Acrobating between the Traditional and the Modern." *Indian Literature* 32: 3 (March): 85-99.

_____. 1989b. "Theatre in India." *Daedalus* 118: 4 (Fall): 331-52.

_____. 1985 [1975]. *Hayavadana*. Translated by the author. Calcutta: O.U.P.

_____. 1983 [1972]. *Tughlaq*. Translated by the author. New Delhi: O.U.P.

Khosla, G.D. 1994. "Sakuntala." In *Tales of Love and War: Stories from the Mahabharat*, 1-11. New Delhi: O.U.P.

Kurtkoti, Kirtinath. 1985 [1975]. "Introduction" In Karnad: v-vii.

Lacan, Jacques. 1972. "The Insistence of the Letter in the Unconscious." trans. Jan Miel. In *The Structuralists from Marx to Levi-Strauss*, ed. Richard de George and Fernand de George, 287-323. New York: Doubledy Anchor.

_____. 1968. *The Language of the Self: The Function of Language in Psychoanalysis*, trans. Anthony Wilden. Baltimore: Johns Hopkins University.

Mann, Thomas. 1961. "The Transposed Heads." In *Stories of a Lifetime*, 214-87. Vol. 2. London: Mercury Books.

Morgan, Thais. 1989. "The Space of Intertextuality." In *Intertextuality and Contemporary American Fiction*, ed. Patrick O'Donnell and Robert Con Davies, 239-79. Baltimore: Johns Hopkins University Press.

Mukherjee, Tutun. 1990. "Persistence of Classical Categories in Modern Indian Drama: Girish Karnad's *Hayavadana*." In *Literature and Popular Culture. A Festschrift for Isaac Sequeira*, ed. R.S.Sharma and others, 131-39. Hyderabad: Cauvery Publications.

Muller, John P., and Willliam J. Richardson. 1982. *Lacan and Language: A Reader's Guide to Ecrits*. New York: International University Press.

Murthy, U.R. Anantha, Prasanna, and Girish Karnad. 1995. "Girish Karnad, the Playwright: A Discussion," trans. Sukanya Chandrasekara. *Indian Literature* 38: 5 (September-October): 127-40.

_____. 1983. [1972]. "Introduction." In Karnad: vii-x.

_____. 1976. "A Note on Karnad's *Hayavadana.*" *Literary Criterion* 12: 2 & 3: 37-43.

Naik, M.K. 1987. "The Limits of Human Power: A Comparative Study of *Tughlaq* and *Caligula.*" In *Studies in Indian English Literature*, 136-45. New Delhi: Sterling.

_____. 1984. "From the Horse's Mouth: A Study of *Hayavadana.*" In *Dimensions of Indian English Literature*, 191-202. New Delhi: Sterling.

Nayak, G.H. 1983. "Karnad's *Tughlaq,*" *Enact* 193 & 194 (January-February): 1-5.

_____. 1973. "Kannada." *Indian Literature Since Independence*, ed. K.R. Srinivasa Iyengar, 93-115. New Delhi. Sahitya Akademi.

Paranjape, Makarand R. 1999. "Metamorphosis as Metaphor: Shape Shifting in Karnad's Plays." Dodiya: 82-91.

Paul, Rajinder. 1971. "Girish Karnad Interviewed." *Enact* 54 (June): 2-6.

Ramamurti, K.S. 979. "Some Aspects of Indian Drama in English with Special Reference to *Tughlaq.*" *Litcritt* 5: 1 (June): 9-22.

Ramanaujan, A.K. 1989. "Is There an Indian Way of Thinking? An Informal Essay." *Contributions to Indian Sociology* 23: 1 (January-June): 41-58.

Ramnarayan, Gowri. 1989. "A New Myth of Sisyphus." *Theatre: The Hindu Folio*. (February, 8): 12-17.

Raykar, Meenakshi. 1982. "An Interview with Girish Karnad." *New Quest* 36 (November-December): 339-42.

Reddy, Bayappa P. 1999. "The Theatrical Representation of History: Girish Karnad's *Tughlaq.*" In Dodiya: 149-55.

Saletone, R.N. 1981. *Encyclopedia of Indian Culture*. Vol. 1. New Delhi: Sterling.

Sarup, Madan. 1989. *An Introductory Guide to Poststructuralism and Postmodernism*. Athens, GA: The University of Georgia Press.

Sharma, Geetha. 1998. "The Play's the Thing." *Graphiti. The Telegraph Magazine* (August, 30): 4-9.

Sharma, P.P. 1978. "On Girish Karnad's *Tughlaq*: An Idealist Gone to Pieces." *New Quest* 10 (July-August): 237-40.

Sharma, R.S. 1978. "Karnad's *Hayavadana.*" *Literary Criterion* 13: 4: 69-74.

Shrotri, Shridhar B., and Majan M. Mulla. 1975-76. "Karnad's *Hayavadana* and Thomas Mann's 'Transposed Heads': A Comparison." *Journal of the School of Languages* (J.N.U.) 3: 2 (Winter): 78-84.

Shukla, A.R. 1999. "Caste and Religion in *Tale-Danda.*" In Dodiya: 289-94.

Wright, Elizabeth. 1984. *Psychoanalytic Criticism: Theory in Practice*. London: Methuen.

Index